ESCAPE FROM DIXIE

by

JOHN BALL

THE STORY OF

LT JOHN LAFLER (85th NY)

CIVIL WAR POW

GOLDSTAR ENTERPRISES
PO BOX 363
WILLIAMSVILLE, NY 14231

PRINTED AND BOUND IN USA

ACKNOWLEDGMENTS

I was lucky to meet Craig Senfield early in my research into the story of John Lafler. He freely shared his vast knowledge and database of the 85th NY Regt. He also told me about Wayne Mahood's *"The Plymouth Pilgrims"* which is the best book available about the 85th NY.

Patricia Monte from the Port O' Plymouth museum supplied several letters that exposed me to the feelings of troops from the "other" side.

My Uncle Ivan Lafler helped me more than he realized when he copied, in longhand, the original John Lafler document back during WW II. I wish he were still here to see the results.

And, most importantly - Rosanne, we survived another book writing!!

Thanks to all of you.

Cover by Colleen Dunne

ISBN 0-929214-08-0

Printed in the United States of America

TABLE OF CONTENTS

INTRODUCTION

The original autobiographical account of the Civil War experiences of my great-grandfather has been handed down through many generations of the Lafler family. The handwritten description was becoming fragile when my uncle, Ivan Lafler, saved it by copying it in longhand while home on furlough during World War II. As I copied his transcription onto my home computer, I thought about how long ago, in time and technology, John Lafler's experiences happened.

After reading his story I wanted to know more about him than his modest writing told. Researching the background information has been a fascinating experience. I was luckier than most people today who begin to research an ancestor's experience in the Civil War. I had a personal account of his experiences, written very soon after his return.

The text of this personal account, included later, is close to the original. I only corrected the misspellings that are certain to occur when something is transcribed twice. I also modified the text slightly to make it more coherent to modern readers. The style of the 1860's allowed great, long sentences with little punctuation and paragraphs that ran for pages.

My original goal was to pass this historical account on to future family generations and add information that would help place it in perspective of the times. Please don't forget for a moment though - this is John A Lafler's story.

J.B.

Chapter One

EARLY DAYS OF THE "GRAND ADVENTURE"

On October 29, 1861, and approximately one month after he turned 21 years old, John Lafler drove the family's horse and buggy from his home in Potter, NY, to Penn Yan. He and his friend and neighbor, 20 year old George Hainer, were anxious to enlist in the volunteer army. The public sentiment for forcefully crushing the rebellion that started six months before at Fort Sumter was building. Everyone was talking about it - even the religious ministers such as John's father, Sidney. Whether one felt the issue was the abolition of slavery or, more commonly, the preservation of the Union, young men wanted to be a part of this patriotic "grand adventure". A common sentiment was "If I don't get in soon, it will be over before I get a chance to participate."

The need to build a large army had become obvious during the summer of 1861 when the Union suffered several defeats, such as at Bull Run. Although the first call for men was for 90 days service, that period was soon changed to three years. This didn't bother John and George as everyone expected this unpleasantness to be over long before that.

Abraham Lincoln had set a quota of volunteers for each state. New York, being the most populated northern state, was originally asked to supply 13,000 troops. By the time the boys from Potter enlisted, New York's quota was over 165,000 men. Influential individuals organized the recruitment for which they expected to receive high military rank in these units.

Uriah Davis, a prominent farmer and lumberman from Bolivar, NY, organized friends from surrounding counties to

Fig 1.   This early photo of John Lafler in a nonregulation uniform was
         probably taken in 1861 before he received his standard issue clothing
         at Elmira. Photographers often supplied uniforms (this one appears
         to be from a militia unit) for photo purposes.

find volunteers to fill a regiment of 1,000 men. A regiment was made up of 10 companies of approximately 100 men each.

John Raines, a lawyer from Geneva, received help from friends in local towns in forming a company. He received help from Thomas Alsop and George Munger, the son of a store owner from Penn Yan, in his effort to raise the needed men. October 29 must have been a well advertised day to sign up as 19 men from Penn Yan enlisted that day. Some would have second thoughts as the departure day arrived - several failed to show. This was not the case with John and George. A few days after enlisting, they were on the train to Elmira.

Also on that train was Wyman Johnson from Waterloo who would become part of the local lore of Yates county. Just prior to leaving to enlist in the army he finished cutting grass with a scythe. He placed the scythe in the crotch of a tree and told his parents he would remove it when he returned. The blade of the scythe is still in the tree today, but only the tip is visible as the wood has overgrown most of it.

Elmira was a military depot, acting as assembly point for volunteers from much of New York state, Pennsylvania, and some areas of Michigan. Here the new recruits were officially mustered into companies and regiments. It is ironic that part of this depot would become a POW camp for Confederate prisoners later in the war.

When John and George arrived at Elmira they were housed in a single story barracks which housed their entire company, Company G. There were 50 bunks in their building, 3 tiers high, most with two men to a bunk. Their buildings were known collectively as "Barracks No. 4". The mess hall contained long tables, each capable of seating a company of 100 men.

The companies that constituted the 85th NY Regt were organized with recruits from general geographical areas as follows:

Company A - Olean, NY

Company B - Canandaigua

Company C - Friendship

Company D - Little Genesee

Company E - Granger

Company F - Black Creek & Friendship

Company G - Geneva (and Penn Yan)

Company H - Wellsville

Company I - Richburg

Company K - Hinsdale

(There were no "J" companies as the letters "I" and "J" were easily confused in the writing style of the mid-nineteenth century.)

At Elmira companies and regiments not up to minimum strength would be consolidated with other regiments. This was probably why the 85th Regiment was made up from troops from so many counties.

The policy of keeping men from the same locality together in a company was probably a good one. It eased the transition from civilian to military life and men would hesitate to shirk their duty in front of friends and acquaintances from back home. Unfortunately, the policy made discipline by commissioned and non-commissioned officers difficult as they were looked upon as friends or were the objects of grudges left over from their civilian relationships. The discipline problem was aggravated by the lack of any military education by the volunteer officers.

Election of officers was one of the first items on a new regiment's agenda. Supposedly, all officers were to be elected. In truth, usually the organizers of the units were assumed to be the officers, especially the ranks above Lieutenant. In some units, the company officer candidates campaigned openly for votes.

Very rudimentary physical exams, often little more than an interview based on several questions by a medical officer, were completed. One physical problem would instantly disqualify a recruit from infantry duty - lack of front teeth. To load a muzzle loading rifle, one had to bite the end from a paper cartridge containing the powder and bullet, pour the powder into the barrel, and ram the bullet to the bottom. Without front teeth, the soldier could not efficiently load his weapon.

A preview of the prevalence of disease in army units was apparent at Elmira. The recruits were mostly from sparsely populated areas. Suddenly they were thrust into crowds of men from many different areas with strains of disease not familiar to them. The importance of sanitation was never understood throughout the war. John Lafler avoided many of the epidemics, especially measles, that raced through the ranks at Elmira several times. He had already had measles as a young boy, so was immune.

The muskets issued to companies A, B, and C were British Enfields. The rest, including company G, received rifles of Belgian manufacture. At the beginning of the war, the Federal stock of weapons included 400,000 rifles and 25,000 pistols, plenty for a short war. Once it was realized that many more soldiers and much more time would be required, government agents traveled to Europe to buy as many guns as might be needed. When they arrived, they found Confederate agents and many from New York and Massachusetts were already buying all available weapons. European governments were pleased to unload surplus guns, regardless of quality, at premium prices. The 85th NY troops considered themselves lucky to get Enfields and Belgian rifles. Two months later, however, they were all exchanged for Austrian muskets to standardize the

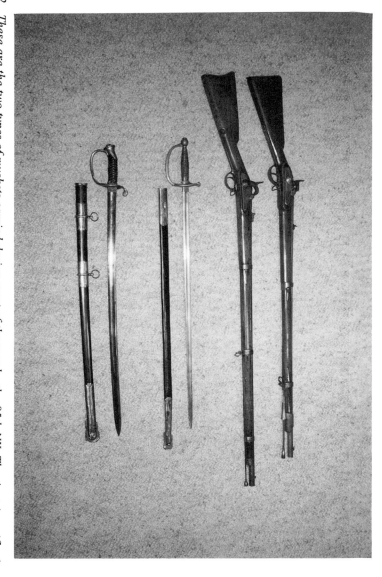

Fig 2. These are the two types of muskets carried during most of the war by the 85th NY. The Austrian rifle (top) was used until Spring 1864. The top sword is a noncommissioned officer's sword. The lower one is an infantry officer's sword.

weapons of the regiment. The average price of a musket in 1861 was approximately $13.

Nine distinct steps were required to fire a muzzle loading rifle. A well trained soldier could fire three aimed shots per minute. This level of proficiency necessitated hours of practice.

When their uniforms were issued the boys from Potter were fortunate they had enlisted in NY state. Many states were not as well prepared with clothing and equipment as New York. Early in the war, soldiers from some northern states were issued whatever uniforms that were available. Some Union troops even wore gray uniforms in the early battles! As a few early Confederate units wore blue uniforms, there was mass confusion as to who was friend and who was enemy. John and George had the eternal soldier's problem of getting a proper fit. There was a lot of trading until each soldier had something passably close to his size. Most of the uniform had to be bought from an allowance of $42. If a soldier needed anything else during the next year it would come from his pay.

Privates were paid $13 per month during most of the war. This was increased to $16 per month in 1864. This wage (about $250 in today's inflated money) was not considered abnormally low as they expected food, clothing, and lodging (such as it was) to be provided. Also, most recruits were accustomed to living frugally.

John was mustered in as a sergeant so his pay was $17 per month and he moved into non-commissioned officer quarters. George became a corporal which was also a considerable improvement over being a private. In Company G, originally with a total of 79 men, there was a Captain (John Raines), a 1st Lt (George Munger), a 2nd Lt (Thomas Alsop), 5 Sgts, 8 Corporals, 64 Privates, 2 musicians, and a wagoner.

Among the last group of 5 men to enlist, on November 25, was 18 year old Alfred Bogert, another Penn Yan enrollee. Recruits had been allowed to go home for Thanksgiving. Alfred (or his parents) may have been persuaded that he was needed in the army by someone already at Elmira.

The daily life at Elmira was dominated by drilling, inspections, maintaining equipment, and guard duty. The several-times-per-day drill was conducted by officers who were learning the military maneuvers by reading the books just before beginning the day's work. This constant drilling was not the glorious adventure the recruits had envisioned before enlisting.

The regiment was ordered to Washington, DC, soon after official mustering on December 2, 1861. Again, some troops decided this was not the life for them and they were not on the train headed south at 7 PM on December 3.

As the train passed through Pennsylvania, the box cars were so cold that some troops attempted to heat them with fires built on the floor. Passing through Baltimore, where Union troops had been attacked a few months before on their way to Washington, they were especially vigilant.

After many stops, they arrived at the New Jersey Avenue station in Washington at 10 AM on December 5. That night they spent their first night in camp tents. The tents were "Sibley tents" and somewhat resembled Indian teepees. Twelve to twenty men slept in each like spokes of a wheel with their feet toward the center. They were usually heated with a conical stove in the center which vented through an opening at the peak. These tents were well known for the odor produced by many men sleeping (in their clothes) in so confined a space.

Army regulations required that the men wash their hands and feet each day and bathe once per week. This regulation was rarely enforced.

Fig 3. This "Sibley" style tent was used to house 12 to 20 men. It is little wonder disease spread rapidly through the ranks in such crowded conditions.

Disease continued to be a chronic problem. Tragically, on January 13 and 49 days after enlisting, Alfred Bogert died. The *"Yates County Chronicle"* newspaper, printed in Penn Yan, contained a letter[1] from John Raines, G Company commander, to Private Bogert's parents notifying them of his death after a two week illness. Private Bogert became the first casualty of Company G.

The weather was generally cold and rainy. At least four hours per day were spent marching. John and George suffered with a general feeling of boredom and desire to get on with the fighting for which they had volunteered.

The camplife proved too much for the unmilitary Col Davis. He resigned with little feeling of loss by his men. LtCol Belknap, also not highly regarded by the troops, replaced him.

The regiment moved to several different campsites from December through March. During that time they were near many historical locations and saw several exciting innovations. They saw the *Monitor* (the iron gunboat that had fought the Confederate *Merrimac*) and the observation hot air balloon of Prof Lowe.

The novelty of military life and new surroundings began to wear away. Rumors circulated that they were soon to see action. Finally, on March 30, 1862, they boarded a steamship headed for Ft Monroe, VA, and their introduction to battle.

---

[1] See Appendix B for complete text of letter.

Chapter Two

VIRGINIA CAMPAIGN OF 1862

The next day the 85th Regt passed Fort Monroe, VA, reputed to be the largest military post in the world, located at the mouth of the James River. They camped near Newport News. They had switched to smaller tents. The officers lived in small, walled tents - a captain had a tent to himself, two lieutenants shared a tent. The enlisted men's tents were made by fastening two 4' x 6' cotton cloths together and stretching them across a pole supported about 3 feet above the ground. Each man carried one of the cloths while marching so two men shared the shelter made from both cloths.

Although there were many rumors of impending heavy fighting, little actual contact with the enemy occurred throughout April.

On April 28, 1st Lt George Munger returned from a recruiting trip back to central New York where he had obtained 9 new recruits.

During May, 1864, the 85th saw action at the siege of Yorktown and at the battle of Williamsburg. It was at the end of the month, at Fair Oaks, that they saw their first major battle.

The following is from a letter[2] by Lt Munger of Co. G describing the battle of Fair Oaks, VA, 31 May - 1 June:

"We were alarmed by heavy firing on our front on the morning of the 29th, also on the 30th, but both proved to be reconnaissances; but on each occasion our forces lost a

---

[2] "Yates County Chronicle", Penn Yan, NY, June, 1862

number of men. About 11 o'clock, of the 31st, I received an order detailing myself and company as pickets for the night and the following day. The men took an early dinner and about one o'clock they were scouring their pieces for inspection, when we received an order from Jeff Davis, in the shape of two shells right in our midst, to "fall in". This is the first order we have received from Jeff, and we obeyed it with alacrity. We marched to the front of our camp into the rifle pits and there lay awaiting the attack. The firing commenced very briskly on our picket line, and as they retreated, two regiments of infantry went forward to meet the enemy and sustain the pickets. These regiments marched up into the slashing, which is about thirty or forty rods in front of the pits.

Instead of the enemy advancing in small force, as we all supposed, it was a desperate effort on their part to break our center and drive us back past the Chickahominy [River]and gain possession of our stores and provisions. These two regiments and the pickets were compelled by the very heavy opposing force, to retreat within our lines, as they were fast being flanked and would soon have been taken prisoners. The 81st N.Y.S.V. took their position in the pits on our left, and two of our regiments on the right of the fort, which was in the center of our pits. As the Rebels came out of the slashing, the battery which was in the fort (Co. A, 1st NY Artillery) shamefully and cowardly left their places - six in number - and fled for a safe place. The enemy were in the mean time pouring in a heavy volley, but not doing us much damage as we were protected. Very soon after the artillerists left, the two regiments in the rifle pits on the right were compelled to retreat, as they were flanked on the right, which fact we were not aware of till our Major saw the rebel flag flying where ours should have been when he gave us the order to retreat. We had retreated back to our camp, when the enemy was driven back on the right and we rallied and went again to the pits. The 2nd Alabama then advanced on us, I suppose with the intention of driving us out of the pits.

They came up splendidly, loading and firing as they came, but our unerring "Austrians" [rifles] were too many for them. Not over one third of the men that came out with the regiment went back. The ground was strewn with them, a perfect windrow about fifteen rods from the pits. They were compelled to retreat and as they went back into the slashing, we looked for our artillery support to mow them down, but they had run, and the curses upon the miserable cowards that went up from our rifle pits were loud and long. The enemy were now out of range, and we rested for we had been in water above our knees for about three hours. We, after a very short time, were ordered to retreat, which we did, but in poor order, as we had suffered severely. The enemy were then flanking us (the 81st and the 56th) both on the right and left, and we had to get out the best we could or be taken prisoners, as the enemy was bringing in heavy forces to support his advance, and we had no support whatever. It was a very poor piece of generalship that we were flanked. Who was at fault I do not know. They never could have taken these pits if we had been properly supported, and this fact so patent to all the men, discouraged them.

After the retreat, I helped one of our company, who was severely wounded in the thigh, to a comfortable place, and then went back for my overcoat, which I succeeded in obtaining, but was compelled to leave everything else. I then undertook to find the remnant of the regiment, but did not succeed. Just at this time I came up to the 96th NYV and LtCol Durkee requested me to help rally his regiment. I took four of my own men as a nucleus, and formed a company of stragglers, who were leaving the scene of action, from different regiments, and placed them on the left of the regiment. This regiment was then filed off to the left to help prevent the enemy from flanking us again, which he was trying hard to do. We halted and lay along side a fence in support of a regiment who had succeeded in driving the enemy back, as found by the dead and wounded rebels who lay thick around us. We found it was a necessity to "lay low" to save our heads. At this time as I was going up to the right of my new company, I received a musket ball in the fleshy part of my forearm. It bled very freely, and an officer standing near offered to take command of the company, and I went to the rear and there found our regiment or about 100 men of it.

The losses of the regiment in the action, including killed, wounded and missing, amounts to near 75. Our loss (that is, Co. G) is as follows: Killed, Corp John Watkins, killed in the rifle pits by a musket ball in the forehead. Wounded, 1st Sgt Alonzo Miller very severely, by a musket ball in the head, and it is supposed he can not live long. He received his wound while lying along the fence with the 96th and after I left. I have not seen him but he has been taken care of as well as possible. Wm. J Dougherty, of Canandaigua, was wounded very severely in the arm supposed by one of our own men carelessly. Josh Bertram, of Geneva, very severely in the thigh. I think he must be dead by this time, as he was left in camp and has had no care up to today, for the reason that our camp was in possession of the rebels, and they had enough of their own wounded to tend to, which they would do first of course. E. Melious, wounded in the thigh severely. He is among the missing and I fear for him; he may be brought in today as the battleground is again in possession of our troops. James Sherman, wounded slightly in the back by a plug from our own artillery, which was firing directly over us, and doing us more damage than they did the enemy. Orrin Sherman was wounded but I do not know what portion of him. Alvah Cole, of Geneva, was wounded severely. He was in camp sick and did not take part in the fight. Alexander P Campbell was struck on the side by a spent ball and bruised some but not as to unfit him for duty. Chester Ellis is missing. Our Col. Belknap was twice taken prisoner and escaped. LtCol Wellman was struck by a ball in the forehead in the early part of the engagement, and will probably not live.

Our Maj RV King, had his knee dislocated by a splinter knocked from a tree by a cannon ball.

The men are almost famished, having not had one complete day's rations in the last three days, which, in addition to standing three or four hours in cold water and lying on the ground these cold, dreary nights, without a thing more than our clothes to cover us, is sufficient to weaken the stoutest man. I cannot muster for duty this morning but twenty men. The remaining seventeen are sick here, and some 5 or 6 went back to the hospital yesterday sick. Two weeks more of such work as we have had the last two weeks, the rest of us will either be dead or unfit for duty."

First Sgt Alonzo Miller and Pvt Alvah Cole died later of their wounds.

The lack of food, shelters and supplies was appalling after the battle. Men slept directly on the wet ground, without food, and weakened by illness. A week later, they began to recover and saw action in the fighting called the "Seven Days Battle".

The 85th was part of the unit protecting 2800 supply wagons during the general withdrawal from the peninsula. They fought at White Oak Swamp, Malvern Hill, and Harrison Landing. In the words of 1st Lt Fay of Company F, "The Union army repulsed the enemy every day and marched away from them every night."[3]

John Lafler served as 1st Sgt after Alonzo Miller's mortal wounding at Fair Oaks. On July 5, it was announced that he was promoted to 2nd Lt to take effect on September 1, 1862. He would soon move to the officer row of tents, leaving his old pal, George Hainer (now a sergeant). Edwin Pierson,

---

[3] "History of the Black Creek Company", Sylvenus Fay, 1910

from Waterloo, became a sergeant and Wyman Johnson, of the "scythe tree" legend, became a corporal.

The regiment was posted to detached duty performing guard duty, drilling, and staying ready for battle when called. Several skirmishes were fought during the next three months, but with no battle casualties. As with most units they had lost more troops to disease than wounds. The regiment size had dwindled so much that Capt Will Clark returned north to recruit more replacements.

Marching orders were received to start marching south on December 5. The original plan was for the 85th to be on loan for 10 days to conduct a campaign on several North Carolina towns, the largest being Goldsboro. During the next few days they had contact with the enemy, took some prisoners, but suffered no casualties. Finally, on December 8, they reached Gatesville just across the border in North Carolina. Here the entire regiment climbed aboard an old steamboat, the *Hussar*, and headed for New Berne[4] , NC.

1st LIEUTENANT

SERGEANT'S Chevrons.

1st SERGEANT.

Fig 4. These are some of the insignia of rank that John Lafler wore during his military career. He was a 1st Sgt for only three months before becoming a Lieutenant.

---

[4] This was often spelled "New Berne" or "Newberne" during the Civil War. Today, it is "New Bern".

CHAPTER THREE

MORE OF THE SAME AT NEW BERNE

Upon reaching New Berne, NC, the men marched to their campgrounds outside the city. The transport ship carrying their haversacks and personal effects had sunk losing all of their military and personal gear. They were forced to use only what they were carrying with them. The garrison troops at New Berne began making jokes about the ragtag regiment that had just arrived. The 85th had an instant dislike for these "Sunday soldiers" who had spent the past year at this supply depot with all its comforts.

The first problems for the tent-dwelling newcomers were swarms of mosquitoes and then bonechilling cold. Those hardships were soon forgotten as, two days after arriving, they headed with several other regiments and artillery support for Goldsboro and the probability of serious fighting.

Kinston, on the road to Goldsboro was strongly defended with three Confederate brigades. After a feint towards the town, the regiment bypassed it by crossing a river on a partially destroyed bridge.

Later the next day a strong skirmish began as an assembly of enemy troops, well hidden in trees, controlled the road. After a strong attack with small arms and artillery, the way was cleared. LtCol Wellman, wounded in the head at Fair Oaks was commanding the 85th. He "lost his head here" and could not stand excitement due to his previous wound. He was sent back to New Berne.

Kinston had been abandoned when they arrived so they burned a bridge and continued toward Goldsboro.

Upon reaching the objective of their expedition, a major railroad bridge at Goldsboro, heavy fighting broke out. The Confederates attacked but were decimated by the Union artillery barrage. The bridge, a major link between Richmond and that area of the South, was burned. The Union troops then headed back to New Berne, reaching it four days before Christmas.

The total loss on the expedition to the 85th was one man who broke his arm at Kinston. The total Union force, however, lost 40 killed and 120 wounded to the Confederates 50 killed, 75 wounded, and 400 captured.

The year 1862 ended with little of note. The 85th Regt received another clothing allowance and settled in for a boring period of guard duty and drilling. They had not been paid for several months and were required to "forage" throughout the town for necessary personal items.

Shortly before the first of the new year, they were officially transferred to the "Department of North Carolina" with MajGen Wessells commanding the Fourth Division.

January and February 1863 brought more of the same routine - drill, guard duty, and occasional excursions into the countryside with little action resulting. At one point, the 96th NY Regt refused to form for parade because they had not been paid for so long. Gen Wessells changed their minds when he threatened to fire on them with artillery guns.

During the middle of March, the Confederates attacked Fort Anderson, a small fort across the Neuse River from New Berne. It was defended by about 300 men from the 92nd NY. They were shelled heavily until reinforcements, including the 85th NY, arrived by boats which they poled across the river while under fire. Miraculously, no one was hurt despite bullets and shell fragments splashing all around them. The Confederates withdrew toward Washington, NC (called "Little Washington") where they laid siege to the town.

The 85th, with eight other regiments, was called upon to break this siege. By the time they arrived the Rebels had left for Virginia.

On May 2, the regiment left New Berne aboard two steamboats, the *Massasoit* and the *Emalie*, bound for the port of Plymouth, NC, on the Roanoke River. The captains had a friendly rivalry from previous encounters and soon engaged in a race. This seemed to shorten the trip somewhat and they arrived at their destination noon the next day.

Fig 5. Modern view of two houses in Plymouth that were built before the war. They were probably damaged during military actions between 1862 and 1864.

Chapter Four

A NEW HOME - PLYMOUTH, NC

The men of the 85th were openly greeted by this small town of approximately 2,000 inhabitants. It had been a shipbuilding town once, but was more recently used as a port for local goods and had several grain mills and a saw mill. It was militarily important as a control of river traffic. Although it appeared to have once been a pretty town, it had suffered badly from the war. It had been taken by the Union in 1862 after a short battle, but a Confederate cavalry raid had caused further damage. It had a garrison of two Massachusetts regiments that were ordered to leave soon after the new troops arrived.

The townspeople were openly friendly to the Union troops. North Carolina had never been as has hard-line secessionist as its neighbors. In 1861 popular sentiment leaned toward not seceding. However, when told they would have to provide troops to fight the upcoming war, they went along with the politicians who had encouraged secession. It would have been difficult to be a Union state surrounded by Virginia, South Carolina, and Georgia! In any case there were many northern sympathizers at Plymouth.

Several men mentioned in their letters home that most of the women were "snuff dippers". They chewed a stick until it looked like a brush, then dipped it into a snuff box. These sticks protruding from the women's mouths were repulsive to every writer.

The men were issued "A" tents and sent to their assigned campgrounds. G Company, with most of the 85th, was assigned to an area west of the town. The first few days were filled with a general cleanup. There was a line of fortification around the town with a main fort centered on the southern (away from the river) side. Soon they set about strengthening the defenses as it appeared they were in for an extended stay.

The 103rd Pa Regt strengthened the main fort, Fort Williams, while the 85th built a fort about a mile and a half to the southwest from the general line of fortification around the town. It was called the "85th Redoubt" or "Fort Wessells".

In June, Col Belknap resigned, much to the relief of the men. They had all accused him of cowardice and complete lack of military knowledge. An unknown officer, Col Enrico Fardella, took over as regiment commander. He transferred from another NY regiment in which he had served after enlisting in New York City. The men came to like this former Italian officer, although initially most hoped that the honor would go to recently promoted LtCol Will Clark.

A change in military attire caused quite a stir among the troops during the middle of June. The entire garrison was forced to switch to regulation hats. These were full brimmed, black felt hats with one side bent up and attached to the crown with a brass eagle pin. To finish it off, it also could be worn with a black feather plume! Although this was the regulation hat, most troops much preferred the standard round cap.

Fig 6. This is the unpopular regulation-style hat the 85th NY troops were forced to wear in June 1863.

The leadership of Company G was changed considerably in June and July. Capt Raines resigned and returned to Geneva to continue his law career. 1st Lt Hiram Coats from Company H was promoted to Captain and replaced him. 1st Lt George Munger had resigned in March[5] . As Capt Coats was soon assigned the duties of Assistant Inspector General of the subdistrict, the command of Company G was essentially left to 2nd Lt John Lafler.

Men sent letters home often and were always pleased to receive them. The Post Office was reliable and delivery was surprisingly fast, considering the modes of travel of the times. Newspapers were especially welcome. Most of the war news in the small town papers arrived in the form of letters from local soldiers in the field.

Although the garrison was not losing many troops due to wounds, disease was taking its toll. Malaria, fevers, diarrhea, and occasionally pneumonia kept the number fit for duty at less than half in some units. The officers were not spared these problems. Captain Nelson Chapin, a 53 year old captain from Allegheny county, was one of the few that stayed healthy. In addition to leading the building of the 85th Redoubt, which he later commanded, he acted as Officer of the Day, Captain of the Guards, and other additional duties nearly every day. He was filling in for other officers who were too sick to take their turn. The 85th lost eight men who died from disease during their stay at Plymouth. Two of them were from Company G.

The camp routine remained much the same throughout the summer and fall of 1863. Mostly it was drill, guard, clean, and strengthen the fortifications. Occasional forays into the countryside for reconnaissance and raiding small camps of Rebels broke up the monotony. Most expeditions were joint

---

[5] See Appendix B for Lt Munger's interesting resignation letter.

Usually the troops rode on boats at night to the closest point to the target. They would then make a surprise attack at dawn and burn all supplies that they couldn't take back to Plymouth. Most Negroes in the attacked towns followed them home.

In August, all but Companies E and K were brought into town. Camp life was as comfortable as could be expected when one lives in a tent. At least sufficient food and supplies were available and personal items could be bought from the local stores and peddlers. The regiment hired two Negro cooks, one of whom was so light skinned that he was occasionally mistaken for Caucasian.

The garrison population at Plymouth was constantly being enlarged by recruits, black and white, from the local area. Many of the blacks were escaped slaves who wanted to fight. The whites were Union sympathizers, draft dodgers, or deserters from the Confederate army. The Confederacy had needed to draft soldiers since 1862 when the initial patriotic rush to enlist had dwindled. The Union, with a much larger population, relied on volunteers until 1863. The draft was particularly unpopular in eastern North Carolina. As the draft age range was increased to 17 - 50 years old to obtain more recruits, the number of locals who joined the Union army at Plymouth grew by as many as 30 per day. 1863 saw the recruitment of the first black soldiers in the North. Two Negro companies were formed at Plymouth (with white officers). The gunboat, *Southfield*, also had about 40 Negro crewmembers

The rebel cavalry had bragged that one night they would get a Negro who was on picket (guard) duty. On an August night, two black soldiers were doing picket duty when a cavalry man came riding through the woods with his sword raised to cut the picket down. He had not counted on there being two men at the post instead of the usual one. As he rode down on one of the guards, the other shot him off his horse. Thus ended that "sport"!

On September 5, John Lafler was promoted to 1st Lt. As Capt Coats was still attached to headquarters as an inspector, John was effectively the company commander. There is no record that he disliked the responsibility, but every muster roll for pay contained his handwritten request for additional pay for commanding the company. This would be $10 in addition to the $113 per month that 1st Lts earned.

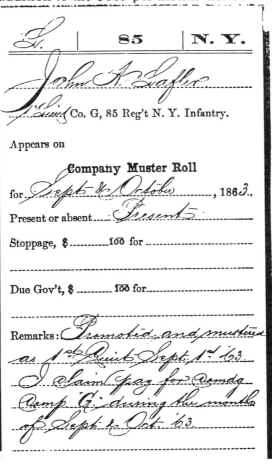

Fig 7. One of John Lafler's Muster Rolls For Pay requesting extra pay for commanding Company G.

On September 5, John's friend, Edwin Pierson from Waterloo, was made an acting 2nd Lt but not "mustered". He could wear the rank and do the duties of a 2nd Lt, but was not officially recognized as one. A year later he would be glad he accepted this "semi" promotion.

As the fall continued there was an increase in enemy activity. Several times, scouting parties discovered small rebel detachments and took prisoners. Rumors began to circulate about a large ironclad gunboat being built upriver.

The Lafler family back home was going through difficult times. John's brother, Ezra, had been drafted in the first Union draft in late summer, an older sister had died of tuberculosis in October, and his parents were becoming feeble in their advanced ages. Ezra probably didn't have the $300 fee (or a substitute to take his place) that he needed to be relieved of his military duty. Finally, he was excused as the "only available son to support aging parents".

By December, talk of reenlistment increased among the troops at Plymouth. In the fall of 1861, when most of the men enlisted, they had signed on for three years. Their time would be up in less than a year. The Union army could not spare all the troops who had enlisted in 1861. It was much more difficult to get recruits in 1863 and the experienced veterans would have been replaced by inexperienced new troops. To help persuade the current troops to reenlist, several plans were implemented. Their patriotic feelings were appealed to, a federal incentive bonus of $400 per man was offered, and a furlough of 30 days would be given to a reenlistee. The reenlistment period was to be three years or the duration of the war.

The $400 bonus would be added to any bonus due from local and state governments. In many cases these bonuses would add up to $700 or $800, roughly equivalent to $15,000 today. It was a strong incentive.

As good as the money appeared though, it was the 30 day furlough that swung many men over to reenlist. Most of the men of the 85th had not been home for two years. They would jump at the chance to go home even if it meant three more years in the army. Besides, duty hadn't been that bad lately and the war should be over well before three years.

The officers also had a reason to persuade the men to reenlist. If a regiment decreased in size too much, it would be combined with other small regiments. There were no other positions for the surplus officers and they would be discharged. The 85th had shrunk from its original 900 plus members to approximately 600.

By January 5, 1864, all the men of three companies, including G, had reenlisted. Most of the others were signing up rapidly. A few had definitely decided against it. This group included the two Phillips brothers who had been engaged to be married when they enlisted. They had promised their fiancees that they would return as soon as possible to get married and refused to postpone it any longer.

Also in January, Company A relieved Company I at Roanoke Island, located several miles downriver. Due to slack discipline, Company I was returned to Plymouth. This would prove unfortunate for them.

Companies C and H left the rest of the 85th in the town when they were posted to Fort Gray, the fort 2 miles up river with several artillery guns and much more pleasant quarters.

On January 11, the required three-quarters quota of reenlistments was reached. The rumors about an enemy troop buildup caused everyone to be anxious about their promised furloughs.

Of great concern was an attack on New Bern by Gen George Pickett (of Gettysburg fame) with 13,000 troops and 14 ships on February 1. They were quite successful until they moved within range of the Union Artillery. Their own artillery was slowly plodding through swamps and muddy roads, but arrived too late to be of help. Gen Pickett withdrew after Union reinforcements, including the 16th CT Regt from Plymouth, arrived. The Rebels had inflicted losses of 100 killed and wounded and had captured almost 300 prisoners.

This caused considerable excitement in Plymouth. It was obvious the Confederacy was becoming serious about retaking the North Carolina coast. Gen Wessells wrote Gen Peck that he needed 5,000 more men to insure the safety of Plymouth. His extravagant request was denied.

The garrison renewed efforts to ensure the fortifications were as strong as they could make them. Natural barriers helped their efforts. The river and a large, swampy island formed a barrier on the north. There were several large creeks around the town that would slow troops and make moving heavy equipment and artillery very difficult if the bridges were destroyed. At the eastern edge of town was a large swampy area thought to provide difficult passage for troops and artillery. As the town was adjacent to the river, the Union gunboats should have been able to control the area even if an attack were launched from there.

There were four forts located outside the main breastworks around the town. The largest was Fort Gray two miles upriver. It had 4 guns, ranging from "24 pounders" to a "100 pounder" (the weight of the shell each fired), to prevent passage of enemy boats from upriver. Fort Wessells was approximately a mile and a half to the southwest of the town. It was made by digging a large area of earth several feet deep. The dirt removed was then added to the log walls. A large ditch surrounded the walls. It was approximately ten feet across and ten feet deep and the dirt from it was added to the walls. Sand bags were piled on top which made the walls nearly 25 feet high from the bottom of the ditch to the top of the wall. The ditch was surrounded by trees positioned with sharpened branches outward. It was armed with a "32 pounder" gun and a "6 pounder" field piece. The other two forts, named Coneby and Compher, were little more than lightly reinforced buildings located to the east and southeast of town.

The main defensive line was a semicircular breastwork enclosing the town stretching from the river on the west, through the south edge, and continued back to the river on the east. Centered on the south side of the line was Fort Williams. This was the headquarters and contained four "32 pounder" cannons. The largest gun, a Parrott gun firing a 200 pound shell, was stationed on the river near the western edge of the town.

There were rifle pits, commonly called "fox holes" today, dug outside the main fortification line. Inside the walls there were holes dug into the walls and areas covered by logs and dirt to protect from airborne shell bursts.

On the river, there were five gunboats containing a total of 32 guns permanently stationed to protect Plymouth.

In early April, the long discussed Rebel ironclad gunboat was finally nearing completion. It had been a struggle to build a boat of this size under the threat of Union attack at any time. To obtain the scarce iron with which to clad the boat, Gilbert Elliott, the 22 year old boat builder, used flattened rails from an idle railroad.

The Union gunboats were under the command of LtCdr Charles Flusser. He devised a plan to deal with the ironclad ram. He would attach a chain between the sterns of the gunboats Southfield and Miami. The river was quite narrow at Plymouth so he would maneuver the attached boats into a "vee" with the opening of it facing upriver. He expected the *Albemarle* would run between the boats and be stopped. The Union boats would then open fire at pointblank range while one of the other gunboats nearby would attempt to disable the rudder of the Rebel boat.

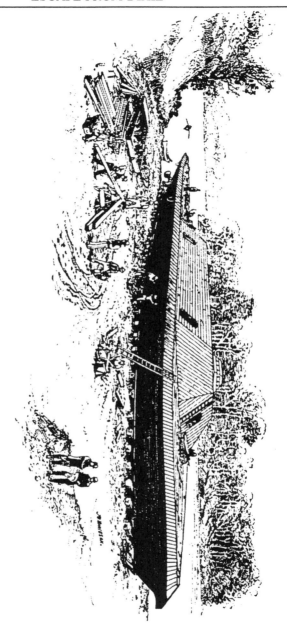

Fig 8. Construction of the Albemarle was accomplished at three different sites on the Roanoke River. The sharpened ram on the bow was normally below the waterline to cause the maximum damage.

The troops felt quite secure in their defensive constructions. George Rogers, a musician in the 85th, wrote his wife that, "We are not 3,000 men here, but a force of 15,000 could not take it." This would prove to be an exaggeration.

Gen Wessells listed the Union garrison manning as:

85th NY	544
16th CT	463
101st PA	409
103rd PA	485
2nd NC	166
12th NY Cavalry	121
24th NY Battery	122
2nd Mass Hvy Art	269
Unattached Recruits	245
Staff	10
TOTAL	2,834

The Confederate troops, under 26 year old BrigGen Robert Hoke, left Tarboro headed for Plymouth on April 15. The force was made up of three brigades totaling 7,000 to 10,000 men. They were commanded by Gen Ransom (8th, 24th, 25th, 35th, and 56th NC Regts), Col Mercer (6th, 21st, 43rd NC Regts & 21st GA Regt), and Col Terry (1st, 3rd, 7th, 11th, and 24th VA Regts). They were supported by sizable cavalry and artillery units. During the night of the 16th, they rested at Foster's Mill, about 16 miles from their destination. At 5 AM on Sunday, April 17th, they started for Plymouth.

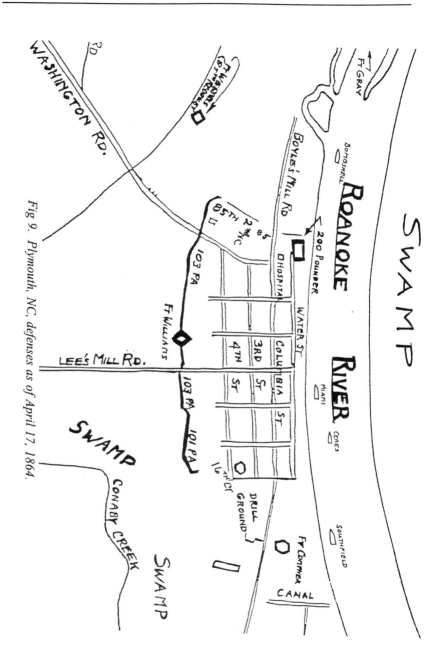

Fig 9. Plymouth, NC, defenses as of April 17, 1864.

Chapter Five

THE BATTLE OF PLYMOUTH, NC

The morning of Sunday, April 17, 1864, arrived with gorgeous spring weather. The men looked forward to a relaxing, light duty day of church services, a short regimental inspection by Col. Fardella, and a dress parade of the entire garrison at 5 o'clock in the afternoon. There would be plenty of time to write home, maybe buy some baked goods from civilian towns people, and prepare boots, rifles and other gear for inspection.

There were rumors of a massing of troops on some point of the Tar river, however, apparently threatening the small town of Washington, NC, 70 miles away. Gen Wessells had received information from the captain of the gunboat *Tacony*, who had just come up the Roanoke river the day before, that there was no enemy buildup on that river between New Berne and Plymouth. As a result, he permitted the modern and heavily armed gunboat to return to New Berne Sunday morning - a decision he would soon regret.

While Col Fardella was inspecting the troops of his regiment, several thousand Confederate troops were only a few miles to the southwest rapidly closing in on Plymouth.

At about 4 o'clock in the afternoon, while the men were contemplating assembling for the parade, the 12th NY cavalry unit patrolling the area a few miles from town were surprised by Confederate cavalry and several troops captured. The reinforcing patrol was forced to return to the town with Lt Russell badly wounded. One picket post was overrun with several troops captured. Among those captured was 1st Lt Charles McHenry, Company B, who had often said he "would like to be on picket duty when the rebels arrive". He was the

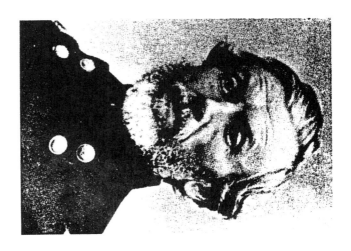

Fig 10. The opposing commanders. BrigGen Robert Hoke was only 26 years old when he was chosen to sweep Union control from North Carolina. BrigGen Henry Wessells was experienced and well liked by his troops.

first officer captured. The skirmish line slowly fell back as a sizable force was assembling on the Washington Road.

The men in town, upon hearing the firing, did not wait for the drum roll signaling them to form up for battle. Their officers soon joined them and they took their planned defensive positions. The following six companies of the 85th were present in town: B, D, E, F, G, and I. Company A was at Roanoke Island, C and H were at Fort Gray, and company K was at the 85th Redoubt (Ft Wessells).

Very soon cannon shells began to explode within the town boundaries. One of the first ones hit the guardhouse of the 85th regiment.

Reinforcements were sent out to support the skirmishers who were slowly being pushed back toward town. The line held for a while, but more and more enemy troops were arriving constantly.

Women, children, and the families of officers were placed aboard the steamer *Massasoit* to seek safety at Roanoke Island.

Gen Wessells sent a message to Gen Peck in New Berne that he was under attack by what loyal civilians reported to be five brigades. They also reported that the iron clad *Albemarle* was as close as Williamston, only a few miles away.

The defensive troops were deployed as follows: the eastern third of the line was manned by the 101st PA and the 16th CT; the center third by the 103rd PA, 24th NY Artillery Battery, and 2 companies of the 85th NY; the western third by loyal NC and Negro troops, several companies (including G) of the 85th NY and 2nd Mass Heavy Artillery. Many of the other civilian Negroes were hastily organized and commanded by Captain Seneca Allen. They carried the older muskets that had been used by the 85th prior to receiving new Springfields a few months before the battle.

As the evening progressed, the Confederate forces applied more pressure. Heavy cannon fire was directed toward Ft Gray but the attackers were unsuccessful in overrunning the fortification. Skirmishing, causing several casualties, continued until about 10 PM. The men "slept on their arms" (in position with full equipment) that night.

The men were up at 3 AM, in anticipation of further attacks. Troops at Fort Gray could see the light of lanterns out on the river as small scouting boats were checking the defensive obstacles that had been placed there to stop the iron clad ram from passing.

At daylight a large cannon battle began and continued throughout the day. The shelling from the gunboats and forts forced the Confederates to move their batteries several times.

A major advance was made upon Ft Gray, probably because it might be a major obstacle to the ram if she came down the river as the Confederate commanders had been promised. Lines of skirmishers attacked and were driven back several times with heavy casualties.

The gunboat *Bombshell* was in the process of communicating with the men at Fort Gray when she was struck below the waterline by a cannon shell and limped back to Plymouth, where she sank at the wharf. The gunboat *Ceres* was reconnoitering upriver from Ft Gray when the battle began. She took several hits, losing 9 men killed or wounded before joining the other boats at Plymouth. The steamer *Massasoit* made another trip to Roanoke Island with noncombatants aboard. Other townspeople preferred to huddle inside their houses, usually in the basements, until the fighting was over.

Nearly continuous skirmishing continued throughout the day along the center of the defensive line. The 85th NY detachment in that area was led by 1st Lt Stephen Andrews. He was required to send for more ammunition and reinforcements throughout the afternoon.

At dusk the Confederates brought nearly all their guns to bear on the town. Although they initially pushed the Union skirmishers outside the town back behind the breastworks, the defense proved too strong and they called off the attack.

Gen Hoke directed his main effort toward the 85th Redoubt (Fort Wessells)[6] . Manning the redoubt were 42 enlisted men of Co K, 85th NY, with their officers, Capt Nelson Chapin, 1st Lt Lucien Butts, and 2nd Lt Spencer Peake, plus 23 enlisted men from the 2nd Mass Heavy Artillery commanded by 2nd Lt Clark. Its armament was only a 32 pounder cannon and a 6 pounder field piece. Against them were assembled the 21st GA Regt and the 21st NC Regt plus several cannons of various sizes.

The fort defenders had traded shells with the enemy during the day with little damage received. However, at about nightfall two batteries were brought up to pour shells into the fort at right angles. Under the covering fire and the darkness, a large column of infantry advanced and completely surrounded the fort. This cut off all communication with the defenders in town. The enemy attacked in force but were stopped by the 10 foot deep ditch around the fort. While preparing to climb the walls of the fort, they were decimated by hand grenades tossed over the parapet by the defenders. This happened three or four times. The main force then passed by the fort toward the town, leaving a few stragglers in the vicinity. Of these, 26 surrendered to the members of the fort. The defenders had lost 1 killed, and 8 wounded (3 mortally). The wounded included the only competent gunners fit for duty.

After a half hour the guns opened up on the fort again. They had been skillfully placed to be hidden from view by the terrain and were very effective. The dirt walls were torn up and the sandbags were broken, destroying the loopholes through

---

[6] See Appendix B for Lt Butt's official report of the defense of 85th Redoubt

which the defenders would fire. During a second cannonading, Capt Chapin was struck in the head by a shell fragment at about 9:30 o'clock. 1st Lt Butts took command of the fort.

Finally, the gunboats opened fire. The shells passed over and exploded far beyond the enemy batteries. The guns in town were more accurate, but two shells landed within the fort causing considerable damage and danger.

Shortly after 10 o'clock, the firing ceased and a demand for surrender was received. The officers present discussed their situation and agreed to accept the demand. Given the lack of ammunition, loss of gunners, and little hope for help from the gunboats, they decided further resistance was useless. The fort was turned over to the 21st GA regiment about 11 PM.

The total casualties of Co K were Capt Chapin (who died the next day), Sgt James Sheldon killed, and 3 enlisted men wounded. The Mass Artillery lost 6 wounded, 2 mortally.

The Confederate attackers lost many killed, including their commander, Col Mercer of the 21st GA Regiment.

Fig. 11. The day after the battle, the victors ordered recaptured slaves to level the 85th Redoubt. This marker is all that remains at the site today.

After capturing the fort, the victors lost no time in adding the fire of the captured cannons to that of their own in pounding the Plymouth defenses. Even with this victory, the Confederate troops were not confident of taking the town without the help of the ironclad ram and no one had heard from it yet. One soldier expected to be ordered back to Tarboro the next morning. The concern was for naught though as the ram at that time was 3 miles upriver from Plymouth. It had stopped prior to reaching the obstacles placed in the river by the defenders to decide how to proceed. The ram's 20 year old designer, Gilbert Elliott, decided to see for himself if passage was possible. In contrast to the report from the scouts the previous night, he discovered that the river had risen just enough for the gunboat to float over the sunken boats and pilings. Capt Cooke headed the ram downriver shortly after 2 AM under a full moon.

The gunners at Fort Gray detected the *Albemarle* as she picked her way towards Plymouth. By staying close to the opposite shore of the river her outline blended in with the heavy foliage. The gunners fired several shots but only produced, as described by one Confederate sailor, "the sound of lead shot being dropped into a metal pail."

Why the 200 pounder cannon at Battery Worth never fired a shot is not certain. Some say the officer in charge lost courage, others say its tackle was fouled so the gunners could not swing it around to fire. The river was only about 1/8th mile wide so a 200 pound cannon ball would have caused heavy damage even to an ironclad gunboat at that range.

The *Southfield* and *Miami* had been returned to their defensive "vee" formation with sterns tied together after having separated earlier to help in assisting Fort Williams and Fort Wessells defend themselves from enemy attacks. The *Albemarle* was so heavy and unmaneuverable, Capt Flusser planned to trap her between his most formidable gunboats and fire at point blank into both sides and, if the hatches were open, follow with small arms fire. The *Ceres* waited a short distance downstream to assist as necessary.

The ironclad ram steamed down the left side of the river gathering speed as though trying to escape outside the two Union boats. At the latest point possible, she swung around and bore down on the wooden *Southfield*, striking her below the waterline. The force of the collision pushed the ram 20 feet into the *Southfield's* hull, causing her to sink immediately. When Capt Flusser's order to fire a 9 inch gun into the ram was not followed quickly enough to suit him, he pulled the lanyard himself. Unfortunately, fragments of the nearby exploding shell flew back at the *Miami*, killing him. Meanwhile, the ram was trapped in the sinking Union boat and was taking on water through portholes as her prey was sinking. Just as the ram appeared doomed, the chains holding the two Union boats together were cut and the ram allowed to back out of the sinking boat's hull. The other boats fled down the river leaving the riverside of Plymouth unprotected. The ram dropped downriver a short distance to stay out of sight of the big gun at Battery Worth but close enough to shell the defenders.

During the daylight of Tuesday, April 19, skirmishing by pickets and shelling by the forts continued. A small unit of the 12th NY Cavalry deployed to the east along the river to prevent any contact between the crew of the *Albemarle* and Gen Hoke. They soon returned to the town where they dismounted and added to the defense of Battery Worth.

The Confederate troops who had attacked Fort Gray were redirected toward the western line of defense of the town - right where much of Company G was entrenched. Casualties on both sides occurred, but no advances were allowed.

Gen Ransom's troops were ordered to the eastern side of town, now unprotected by Union gunboats. After struggling across swamps and creeks, they finally reached the river near midnight, completing the encirclement of the town.

Fig 12. Probably the most important event that sealed the fate of the Plymouth defenders was the sinking of the Southfield. After driving the Union gunboats away, the Albemarle had uncontested control of the river.

The previous three days had been long and tiring. Fighting all day and withstanding shelling most nights had kept both sides dog tired.

There is a difference of opinions described in reports made later about the morale of the defending troops the night of April 19. Gen Wessells stated that, due to the nearly hopeless situation of being surrounded by a larger foe, no support from the gunboats, and the impossibility of reinforcements arriving in time to help, the men were very discouraged. Many of the loyal North Carolina troops slipped across the river during the night as they knew what treatment they would receive if captured by the Confederates. Many had deserted from the very units they were facing. On the other hand, reports from two enlisted men state that the troops were in good spirits even though they recognized the difficulties they faced. Some visited the sutler (peddler) to buy items they might need the next day. One account even described the troops singing "to suit their fancy." They were as prepared as possible for whatever the next day might bring.

At daybreak of April 20, Ransom's troops were ready to attack from the east. They assembled and waited for the signal rocket from Gen Hoke to move out. First there was a diversionary skirmish started at the west end of town and shelling by artillery and the *Albemarle*. Soon the rocket was fired. The advance by Ransom's brigade started slowly. One account by an enlisted Confederate soldier mentioned coming upon a herd of cows. They decided to drive these cows ahead of them as a living barricade. They soon came to a canal across their path. At this point, "as these bovines had no reputation of courage to uphold, they turned and ran for the rear through our ranks." The mass of troops picked up speed and were soon double quick advancing toward the defenders. The Union troops were overwhelmed by the numbers and ferocity of the attackers and were forced to fall back. With the eastern line broken, enemy troops poured into town primarily along the

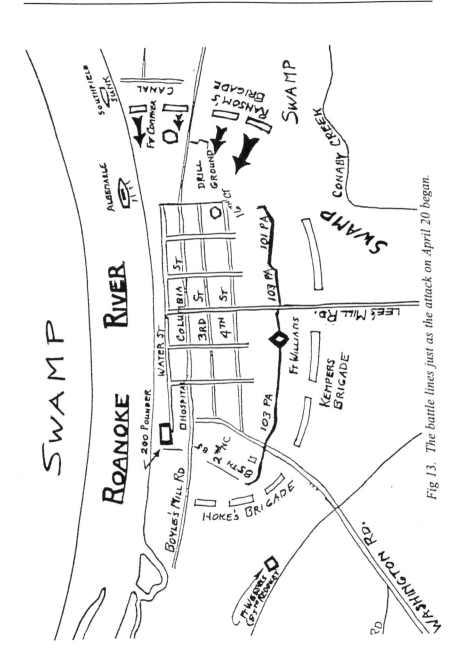

Fig 13. The battle lines just as the attack on April 20 began.

river. They soon overran Battery Worth, removing the threat of the big gun. Some loyal NC troops were stationed in the ditch surrounding it, but they were not effective because the depth of the trench was three feet more than most men's height!

Gen Hoke requested a meeting with Gen Wessells. He demanded an immediate surrender. Gen Wessells was impressed with the young general's bearing, but refused to give up his command.

Within an hour the Confederates opened up with a terrific cannonading from all directions. The only way to survive was to stay inside Fort Williams or "bombproofs" (covered holes dug into the ground). When the firing slacked off, infantry troops continued their assault by sweeping through the streets and fighting the entrenched troops from the rear of their originally planned defensive line. There were so many attackers that one soldier said it was "like firing into a flock of blackbirds[7] ." There was no need for careful aim. Still, one company at a time was forced to surrender.

Some of the colored troops exchanged their uniforms for civilian clothes. It would be better to be taken for a slave than a Negro with a gun. One of the white officers who had been recruiting and leading them put on a private's uniform so he wouldn't be recognized if he were captured. The lieutenant refused to deny his position and later defied his captors. He was imprisoned with his black troops.

The color guard of the 85th, seeing that defeat was imminent, tore up the flag into small six inch strips and distributed them among the men nearby. At least it would not be captured intact.

After conferring with as many officers as available, Gen Wessells consented at approximately 10 AM to hoist the white flag signifying the surrender of the entire post and all its contents. By noon, most detachments had gotten the word and

---

[7] "Charlie Mosher's Civil War", Mahood

laid down their weapons. The Fort Gray detachment was the last to get word of the defeat and subsequently surrendered.

The commanders at Headquarters in New Bern belatedly attempted to rush 800 men by steamboat to reinforce the garrison at Plymouth on the morning of April 20. Unfortunately, the fate of the defenders was already sealed.

The statistics of the battle are not well documented. The entire Union garrison was captured so they had no records and the victors had no incentive to precisely determine the numbers that might interest future historians. Gen Wessells listed 2,834 Union killed, wounded, and missing. Others list only approximately 1,600 as having been at a roll call the morning of April 17. Possibly this number only included infantry troops and may not have included the loyal North Carolina troops. The largest unit was the 85th NY with 450 combatants. The number of Confederate troops was estimated at 7,000, 12,000 or 15,000, depending on which source is used.

Casualty estimates also vary widely. Union sources estimated their killed and wounded at from 150 to "less than 800"; the enemy's at 850 to 1700. Confederate sources estimate the Union killed and wounded as 250 to 500 ; their own as 525 to "many".

The 85th NY Regt lost 1 officer and 12 enlisted men killed. G Company lost 3 killed: Sgt Wyman Johnson (who left the scythe in the tree), Cpl Benjamin Gay, and Cpl Martin Insco. Four others were captured and never heard from again.

John Lafler, acting as company commander, escaped injury, but Lt Pierson was wounded twice - in the shoulder and arm. Capt Coates was wounded in the face inside Fort Williams with Gen Wessells and his staff.

The conquering troops were ecstatic. The garrison supplied them with supplies for several weeks. They consumed more food in the first few days than they had had in weeks.

The Confederate commanding officer, Brig Gen Robert Hoke was promoted to Maj General due to his success at Plymouth.

In the evening of the victorious day, patrols were sent to the swamp across the river to search for Negroes and deserters who had joined the Union army. Throughout the night rifle shots were heard, probably as a result of these escapees being discovered. There was a report of an organized massacre of all Negro troops, but this has been mostly discounted. Some may have been shot, but no mass anihalation has been confirmed[8].

There is a report however of a unit of North Carolina troops forming along a road over which the prisoners marched in two rows. The Confederate troops removed any prisoners they recognized as deserters. At least eight were later court martialed and executed[9].

Despite the harsh treatment of a few, most of the captives were treated better than expected. They were allowed to keep most of their personal belongings, unlike prisoners of many other battles. This would help them later in prisoner of war camps.

The parishioners of the Plymouth Episcopal church donated wood from their church pews to make coffins for the dead of both the Union and Confederacy.

The day after the surrender, the captured troops were given rations for 4 days (forty hardtack crackers and a pound of pork) and marched out of Plymouth. On the 24th, they reached their destination, Tarboro. On the way they were treated surprisingly well by their guards, the 35th NC Regt.

---

[8] "North Carolina Historical Review" - April 1995 - Massacre at Plymouth
[9] Ibid.

Fig 14. The Episcopal church of Plymouth as it appears today. After the battle, its members donated hardwood pews to be cut into lumber for coffins for soldiers of both sides.

The next day, April 25, they were packed into box cars - 50 to a car - to continue their journey. Some of the cars had been used to transport cattle and had not been cleaned. This must have made for a long trip! Each car had 12 guards - 6 inside and 6 outside on the roof. The doors of the cars were opened only about a foot. It was suffocatingly hot and there was not room enough for all to lie down at once.

During the next 5 days they passed through Wilmington, Charleston, Savannah, and Macon. At each major stop the guards tried to find authorities who could incarcerate the officer prisoners but no one had the facilities and manpower to accept them.

At one point they crossed a repaired bridge that the 85th had burned in December, 1862. On this trip they were often called "Plymouth Pilgrims", a name that remained with them throughout their prison stay. Also on the trip, some of the troops traded insults with a railroad engineer who had been born in Penn Yan, the village where John Lafler had enrolled![10]

On April 30, they arrived at the notorious Andersonville Prison, not far from Plains, Ga. The rail trip took 5 days because the condition of the southern railroads was so bad a 12 mph speed limit was in effect.

The commander of the prison, Capt Wirz, refused to accept the officers because "he didn't have facilities for them". One of the prisoners already at Andersonville was the brother of Company F's 1st Lt Fay. Lt Fay was not allowed to see him but sent some money and clothes in to help him. Unfortunately, the brother later died and was buried there.

It was a sad time for both officers and men to be separated after experiencing so much together in the previous two and a half years. Of the approximately 400 enlisted men from the 85th NY who marched into the prison, 265 would not survive the war.

---

[10] *"Plymouth Pilgrims"*, Mahood

The officers were put under guard in a church near the railroad. The next morning they climbed back on the train bound for Macon, Ga. Arriving in the afternoon of May 1, they were marched to the fairgrounds where they were issued tents. The prison stockade for officers at Camp Oglethorpe was not yet built.

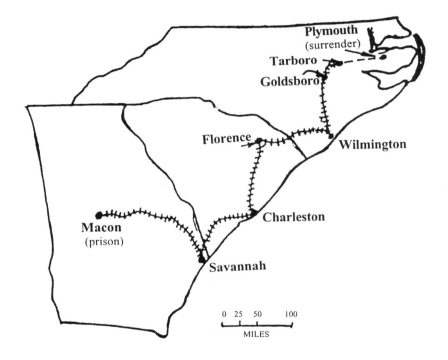

Fig 15. The long trip of the "Plymouth Pilgrims" to Macon, GA.

Fig 16. The stockade at Camp Oglethorpe, Macon, GA. It would not look as spacious with 1200 prisoners living there!

The following four chapters are the personal account by John Lafler of his imprisonment and escapes from Confederate prison camps.

LIFE IN DIXIE
by
John A Lafler

I was taken prisoner by the Rebels at the surrender of Plymouth, NC, April 20, 1864. Immediately after the surrender, we were marched to Tarboro, NC. We took transportation on the cars,[11] our destination being Macon, GA. We passed through Goldsboro, Wilmington, Florence, Charleston, and Savannah, arriving at Macon on the 30th day of April.

Immediately on our arrival we were marched to Camp Oglethorpe, situated just outside the city where we were furnished with a limited supply of tents. We remained in this camp about three weeks, during which time the Rebels were preparing a stockade. When it was completed we were transferred into it - in company with officers from Libby Prison, numbering in all about twelve hundred officers.

Our rations were rather short - consisting of one pint of corn meal, a small piece of bacon, a little sorghum, and a spoon full of rice per day. Our treatment was very severe.

Tunneling was commenced, but we were unsuccessful, as there were traitors among us who informed the Rebels of what we were attempting.

---

[11] The Civil War term for travelling on a train.

It being warm weather, I decided to convert my blanket into a Rebel uniform to evade the guards if an opportunity to escape arose.

On the 28th day of July, we received orders to be ready to move the next morning at 3 o'clock. At the appointed time we were marched to the depot where we took transportation on the cars, our destination being Savannah, GA. My Confederate uniform was nearly hidden from view by a large blue overcoat, which I had put on for that reason.

When we arrived at Millen, which is at the junction of the Ga. Central and Savannah railroads, the train stopped about thirty minutes. Here the guards were allowed to go to a well nearby to fill their canteens with water. This was my time to go.

Accordingly, I took off my overcoat and gave it to Lieut. Pierson of my company requesting him to keep it until I called for it. I took my canteen and went to the door. I told the guard that I wished to fill my canteen at the well. He did not object, and when I had passed him I felt like a new man. Little did I know what I would encounter in making my way to Sherman's army which was near Atlanta, Ga, about three hundred miles away.

I went to the well and filled my canteen and then walked a little way into the bushes and secreted myself. Soon the train moved on and I was left behind.

I now took a small map from my pocket which I had obtained from one of the officers before leaving Macon. On looking it over and finding where Atlanta lay, I decided to follow the railroad in the direction of Macon until I reached Sandersville, a small town about sixty miles from Macon. I would then pursue a northwesterly direction until I reached Sherman's army.

I went to a "soldiers home" nearby and inquired what time the train from Savannah would arrive. The proprietor informed me that there would be a freight train at seven o'clock.

When the train arrived, I went to the conductor and informed him I was a private in the 5th Ga Infantry, that I had been detailed to guard Yankee prisoners from Macon to Savannah, and that I was taken ill before arriving there. My Captain ordered me to stop and go back to Macon on the first train up from Savannah and report to the surgeon of my regiment. All this availed me nothing; he would not allow me to get on the train without a pass as his orders were very strict regarding soldiers.

I watched my opportunity - determined not to give up. When the train was starting, I climbed up on the side of the car with the intention of getting on top. I should not have been able to do it had it not been for a negro boy who was on top of the train. Seeing my condition, he came to my rescue and assisted me.

The train ran about 25 miles and switched off until morning. When the train stopped, I came down and followed the Negro to a freight car which I occupied until about midnight. At that time I was discovered by the man that had charge of the switch and he took me into custody.

I followed him to his little shanty. He kept a close watch over me for a while but just before day he got careless and I made my escape from him.

I then took up my quarters in another freight car, closed the doors and remained quiet until the train arrived at Sandersville. I intended to leave the train when all was quiet. I got out of the car and went to a house nearby to fill my canteen.

I got into conversation with an old planter who informed me that the Yankee General Stoneman, at the head of a large cavalry force, had struck the Central Railroad at Jordan, ten miles from Macon. He had destroyed it for about thirty miles and had burned the bridge on the Oconee River which was only eight miles from Sandersville. I thought perhaps Stoneman would march on Milledgeville, the capital of the state.

After leaving the railroad, I decided to go in that direction, hoping I would fall in his way and thus be rescued. I stopped two or three times during the day to get something to eat, telling the people a good story. I inquired if the Yankees were expected that way and expressed some fear of being captured by them.

About ten o'clock in the evening, while passing through Buffalo Swamp, I was surprised and captured by some Rebel pickets. I did not see them until I was so close to them that it would have been folly to attempt to escape from them. They had been posted there to give the alarm when Stoneman made his appearance.

They wanted an explanation which I immediately proceeded to give them. I informed them that the company to which I belonged had been detailed to guard Yankee prisoners from Macon to Savannah and when we arrived at Sandersville on our way back to Macon we learned that the Yankees had burned the bridge over the Oconee River. We were obliged to wait at this place until the bridge could be rebuilt. I obtained permission of my captain to go to Milledgeville to visit some friends and, after finishing my visit, I was to take transportation on the cars to join my regiment at Macon.

This explanation appeared satisfactory to all except one. He appeared suspicious that my story was not altogether founded upon facts. If it would have not been for him, I would have been allowed to continue my journey that night.

He finally took me to his house which was about two miles distant. In the morning he would go with me to Milledgeville and satisfy himself that all was right. I was kept in a small room during the night, guarded by two Rebels and some dogs.

On the following morning he informed me he could not go to Milledgeville. He had decided to take me back to Sandersville and have my case investigated. I had the honor of riding in a buggy with an officer from General Lee's army, guarded by three mounted men.

We arrived at Sandersville about noon. I was immediately turned over to the enrolling officer. I saw there was no escape now as there were many Rebel soldiers there. I decided to tell the truth to avoid being taken as a spy. I told them I was an escaped Union prisoner which they were not inclined to believe because I was wearing a Confederate uniform.

The enrolling officer asked me what General Burnside had done with two Confederate soldiers that he captured in the Union lines wearing Yankee uniforms. I told him I believed he hung them. He then asked me what reason I had to expect treatment as a prisoner of war.

While this conversation was going on, quite a crowd had gathered around us and began to be quite *clamorous. Some said, "Hang him - he is one of General Stoneman's spies"; others said, "Give him to us. We will take care of him so that he will do no more harm." The enrolling officer saw by this time that things were getting quite serious. Fearing that he might be brought to account for the treatment I received while in his charge, he immediately sent for the officer who had charge of us when we left Macon.*

Immediately after the officer arrived from Savannah, the enrolling officer gave him my name, rank, and regiment. As soon as the officer saw me, he said I had been a prisoner at Macon and had escaped between Macon and Savannah. This explanation satisfied them that I was not one of General Stoneman's spies. I felt somewhat easier.

I was placed on a train in the charge of two trusty guards who had orders to go to Savannah with me and turn me over to the officer commanding the prison at that city. The conductor insisted on locking me up in a freight car as he did not want me to ride with the passengers. This the sergeant refused to do, fearing I might escape and he would be held accountable; consequently I was allowed to ride with the passengers. I took a seat by myself. One of the guards occupied the seat in front of me and the other the seat behind me.

I listened to an interesting conversation among the passengers regarding Stoneman's raid. They told how narrowly they had escaped being captured and what depredations the Yankees had committed. I slept with one eye open until about two o'clock when I discovered that my guards were both asleep.

When the train arrived at the next station they were still sleeping. I arose from my seat and walked carefully out of the car. I took up my quarters in another car without being discovered by my guards. I did not think it best to leave the train for fear I might be caught with dogs as soon as I was missed. I decided to go to Savannah and then attempt to reach Fort Pulaski, only sixteen miles below Savannah, which was held by our forces at that time.

By the time we arrived at the next station, the guards had missed their charge and set about searching the train. After a short search I was discovered and taken in charge again. They were considerably excited. I think they managed to keep their eyes open the remainder of our journey.

g 17. The route of the escape from the train between Macon and Savannah.

Initially, the prisoners were treated well at Macon. General Cobb welcomed them with a proposition that, if they would pledge their word not to escape, he would give them the freedom of the city and better rations. The men realized, however, that to accept would free a company of Confederate soldiers to fight instead of guard them. It would also prevent them from escaping even if Union troops were near. The sanctity of a man's word was strong in 1864, even in wartime. No one accepted the offer.

The prison at Macon was built on fairgrounds 1/4 mile east of the city. It was surrounded by a wall 10 to 12 feet high that had a narrow walkway for guards to patrol. There was a low picket fence inside that acted as a "deadline". Anyone caught between the deadline and the exterior wall was to be shot without warning.

At first, there was one large building that held a small percentage of the population. Later, several smaller barracks were built, but never enough to hold everyone. Prisoners built their own shelters or dug under the buildings for protection from the sun and rain.

Water for the prisoners was supplied by a stream that flowed under the wall, through part of the grounds, and back out under the wall. Although not really sufficient, and soon contaminated, it was probably better than many of the southern prisons had.

If they could afford the prices, the prisoners were allowed to buy supplies from civilians who came to the prison gate. In June, 1864, the exchange rate for Confederate money was 1 US "greenback" = 4 1/2 Confederate dollars. The price of a gallon of molasses was $25 to $35 confederate.

Daily rations were minimal, consisting of: 1 pint cornmeal, 2 oz bacon preserved in wood ash instead of salt, 1 oz peas or rice, and 1/2 tsp. salt. Every five days they were also given 1/2 pint of syrup (sorghum) and 1 tablespoon of soft soap. The cornmeal was often baked into loaves called "pones". They simply mixed the meal with water and salt and baked it in a fire for 1/2 hour. As meager as the rations were, they would later be considered plentiful.

Utensils (forks, spoons, and dishes) were very scarce. Men often drew their rations in caps, socks, tied off pants legs, etc.

Each day a few men were escorted outside the prison to obtain firewood. Trash was picked up each day by Negroes who also brought in Macon newspapers. The most accurate war news was brought in by new prisoners.

Illness was a large problem. Diarrhea/dysentery was common and there was no medicine available to treat it. Scurvy was prevalent due to the lack of fresh vegetables. Contagious diseases were sometimes introduced to the prison by newly captured prisoners.

Occasionally, a man would be shot for no apparent reason. No one reported any disciplinary actions taken against a guard for doing this.

Two weeks after the Plymouth prisoners arrived, several dozen officer prisoners from Libby prison in Richmond were added, bringing the total to approximately 1200 by the end of May, 1864. The prison population peaked at 1600 or over 1700, depending on which source you use.

The tunneling John Lafler mentioned may have been prompted by the officers from Libby prison. One hundred nine prisoners had escaped from there on February 3, 1864, by tunneling. Fifty-nine of them made it to Union lines.

Digging tunnels without arousing the suspicion of the guards was difficult. The general plan for constructing an escape tunnel began with digging a vertical shaft 6 feet by 6 feet at the surface. At the depth of 1 foot it was decreased to 4 feet by 4 feet, creating a shelf as shown in the figure on next page.

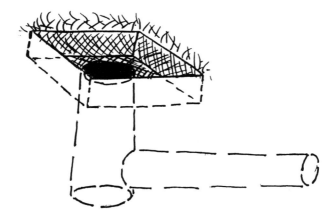

Fig 18. The tunnels at Camp Oglethorpe were constructed in this manner at night. Before morning, they were covered by boards and dirt.

From the bottom of this shaft the horizontal tunnel, just big enough to pass the largest escapee, extended under the prison wall far enough to prevent detection by the guards if escape was possible. A digger could only tolerate about 20 minutes in such close quarters. Straps and ropes were attached to remove the digger if he fainted.

Keeping a shaft at the correct depth was difficult. One tunnel was exposed when a grazing cow fell through because the tunnel was dug too close to the surface!

The men removed the dirt in stockings, pantlegs, and small bags of any kind. To dispose of the dirt without the guards knowing, they dropped some into the sink (the Civil War term for latrine) or in the stream that ran through the prison.

In the morning, the diggers placed boards across the vertical shaft on the 1 foot wide ledge. After dirt was placed over the boards, the opening was hidden so well that a guard could walk across it without discovering it.

Maj Gen Wessells was the highest ranking prisoner at Macon. He had been confined in Libby prison for two weeks after the Plymouth battle before being transferred to Danville and then Macon. He was paroled and returned to New York in August, 1864.

In mid-June, the 50 highest ranking officers, down to half the Majors, were transferred to Charleston, SC, to prevent further firing on the city by Union gunboats. It didn't work, but caused a lot of bad feelings in the North. It was a flagrant violation of an agreement signed by both sides earlier in the war.

Several escapes were attempted from Macon. A few prisoners sneaked out one night through the hole in the fence where the spring entered the camp area. The last man made a noise that alerted the guards, but they all were successful in evading recapture.

One resourceful officer made his escape by hiding in a sutler's box that had been used to bring supplies into the prison for sale.

Lt H. Bader, 29th MO Vols, made a jacket and pants from a gray, woolen blanket and walked out with the guards one evening. He was recaptured. He persevered, however, attempting 5 more escapes!

Another officer, described as a "young officer from Massachusetts" tried this same trick, but was unsuccessful because his shirt was too clean! This information came from two different sources so may really have been the same incident.

As Sherman approached on his "march to the sea", the Confederates decided to move the prisoners to preclude their liberation. Three groups of prisoners, totaling 600 men, were sent to Savannah on the morning of July 28 and dawn of July 29 (when John left).

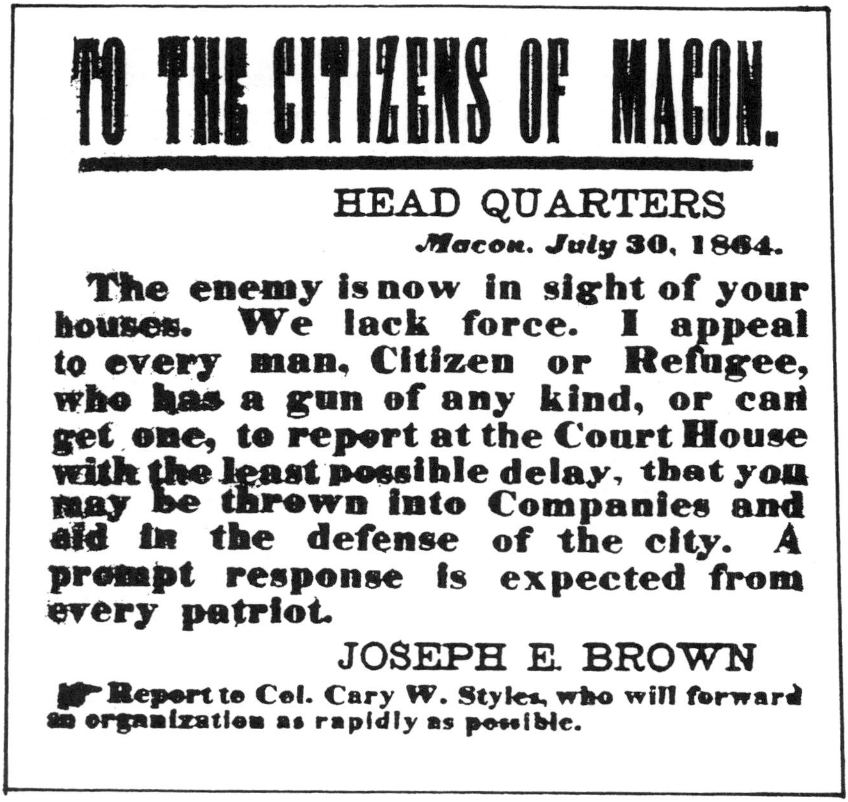

TO THE CITIZENS OF MACON.

HEAD QUARTERS

Macon. July 30, 1864.

The enemy is now in sight of your houses. We lack force. I appeal to every man, Citizen or Refugee, who has a gun of any kind, or can get one, to report at the Court House with the least possible delay, that you may be thrown into Companies and aid in the defense of the city. A prompt response is expected from every patriot.

JOSEPH E. BROWN

☞ Report to Col. Cary W. Styles, who will forward an organization as rapidly as possible.

Fig 19. This handbill was distributed the day after John Lafler left for Savannah. It apparently refers to Gen Stoneman's cavalry raid.

Some of the prisoners made saws from knives with the idea of sawing through the floorboards of the boxcars on the way to Savannah. The first group made plans to overpower the guards and make a mass escape. When the time came though, enthusiasm disappeared and no escape resulted.

Chapter Seven

ESCAPE NO. 2

We arrived at Savannah on the morning of the 1st day of August. I was immediately turned over to the officer commanding the prison, who conducted me to the stockade where the Union officers were confined. About noon a Rebel officer and two of the guards came to me and informed me that I must go with them to headquarters.

After going to headquarters, I was sent to the guard house at the barracks where I was placed in close confinement. Here my rations were very short. Had it not been for the colored friends, I should have suffered very much from hunger. They managed to smuggle some provisions through the iron bars in the window. I was allowed to go into the yard once each day to get some water, accompanied with a guard. The yard was surrounded by a brick wall about ten feet high except at the entrance which was strongly guarded.

While I was after water, I discovered a place where I thought I could climb over the wall and escape if I could get out of sight of the guard. Before making an attempt, I arranged with a darkey to take my blanket, haversack, and canteen through the window and leave them with a colored lady who had done my washing. I promised to call for them after making my escape.

On the 29th day of August, after making all necessary preparations, I asked the guard to let me get some water. The guard told me I could go to the cook house on the opposite side of the building. As soon as I was out from under the eye of the guard I ran to the wall and climbed over it without being discovered.

I ran about half way through the city when I discovered a negro looking out of his window. I informed him I was an escaped prisoner and wished him to conceal me in his house until dark when I intended to leave the city. He conducted me into a small room where he thought I would be safe.

After dark I started to go to the barracks after my blanket when I was met by a colored man who informed me that they were making a thorough search for me. They had attempted to bribe the old lady who had charge of my blanket - telling her that if she would give the alarm when I came after my blanket (so they might surround the house and capture me) they would give her one hundred dollars. She told them she knew nothing about me.

After receiving this information, I did not think it best to attempt to get out of the city until the excitement was over. The next morning I went to the house and occupied my old quarters of the day before.

About ten o'clock the guards came to the house and inquired of the colored people if there were any white men in the house. They informed the guards that there were none. This was not satisfactory and they immediately set up a search for me. There was no latch on the door by which my room was entered; consequently, it was not discovered by them. After they had satisfied themselves that there were no Yankees in the house they passed on to the next.

After they had gone, I hid under the house, deciding this would be a safer place in case the house was searched again. The ground was damp and cold which made it very unpleasant.

After I had remained in this place about two hours, I came out to search for a better place. I went to the outskirts of the city where I found some colored people at work. They advised me to stay with them until dark and, in the meantime, they would prepare some rations for me.

I learned from the colored people that the river in the direction of Fort Pulaski was strongly picketed. A number of deserters had been captured while attempting to reach our forces there. I did not think it best to go in that direction. I decided to attempt to reach Sherman's army at Atlanta by the same route I had taken before.

At dark, when I had received my rations and bade the darkies goodbye, I started for the Central Railroad which I reached just outside of the city. This I took as my guide.

As I was crossing the highway about 20 miles from the city, I heard some horsemen rapidly approaching me. I lay down in some bushes and they passed on without discovering me. I now discovered a light ahead of me which I succeeded in avoiding with some difficulty. I afterwards learned that it was a picket post. At daylight I saw by the mile posts that I had walked 25 miles.

I went into a swamp near the railroad where I hid until dark, not thinking it safe to travel during the day. I came onto the railroad as soon as it became dark enough that I thought I would not be discovered. This night I walked about the same distance that I had the previous night, placing me about 50 miles from Savannah.

I decided to get a ride on the cars which I thought would be a great help to me. I hid in a swamp during the day. As soon as it was dark, I started for the depot. While on my way to the depot, I learned from an old lady that the train going west would arrive at the depot at about 9 o'clock.

I secreted myself behind a pile of railroad ties until the train arrived. After I approached on the opposite side from the depot, and entered a freight car and closed the doors after me, the train moved on. I was soon carried to Millen, a distance of 40 miles, at which place the train stopped about 30 minutes.

I soon discovered that my car was to be occupied with Rebel soldiers on the way to the front. As a light approached the car, I got out on the opposite side; it being very dark, I was not discovered. I learned that they were just from the hospital and belonged to different regiments in the army. I concluded I could occupy a place among them without being detected. Accordingly, as soon as the light was removed, I entered the car again and the train moved on.

The Rebels soon fell into a sound slumber. While they were enjoying their repose, I exchanged haversacks to have a larger one. I filled it with their rations, leaving my haversack in exchange for theirs. I also confiscated a canteen.

We arrived in Sandersville at 3 o'clock in the morning. I had ridden a distance of 80 miles which was quite a help to me.

I immediately left the train at this place and started in the direction of Atlanta. I passed through Sandersville and hid during the day in the bushes about a mile from town.

I came on the road again soon after dark. I soon discovered that I had taken the wrong road. After about one hour's travel, I arrived at an extensive plantation. The Negroes informed me there was a path which would take me onto the other road which was about 4 miles distant. The path was very dim and I soon lost it entirely. I was now obliged to use the North Star as my guide. About 12 o'clock it became cloudy and I was forced to lay down in the dreary forest until daylight.

As soon as I could see, I took a small compass from my pocket and started in a northerly direction. It was a very rough country and I had great difficulty in making my way through the swamps. I tore my clothes among the brush and thorns which were very thick in places. I traveled in this manner until noon when I discovered another plantation.

I went as near to the house as I dared, hoping I might draw the attention of one of the negroes and learn something in regards to the road. I was discovered by a white boy who immediately gave the alarm.

I had not gone very far when I heard some dogs behind me. I was soon overtaken with a party of militia and a pack of hounds. I was obliged to surrender. One of the party took me to his house and kept me until the next morning when I was taken to Sparta and confined in jail.

Fig 20. The route after the escape from Savannah, GA.

In general the conditions, grounds, medical care, and rations were better in Camp Davidson in Savannah than in the Macon prison. Most prisoners were housed in tents in a yard next to a hospital. Unfortunately, the water smelled of sulfur. This was not unique to the prison - much of the well water in the city smelled the same.

Daily rations here consisted of: 1 qt cornmeal, 1 pt rice, 1 lb beef, 1 tspn salt, 1 tspn vinegar, and a piece of hard soap. Occasionally, salt pork was substituted for the beef.

Groups of prisoners formed into small cliques and tended to stay by themselves. They were incensed to see slaves, men and women, forced to dig a new sink (latrine). Some of these slaves were so light colored they were nearly Caucasian.

By September, the exchange rate of Confederate dollars to Union "greenbacks" was up to 10 to 1.

The guards were from a Georgia regiment commanded by Col Wayne. Although they discovered several partially completed tunnels, they could not prevent a few successful escapes.

On September 13th, two weeks after John Lafler's escape, the remaining prisoners were transferred to Charleston, SC, before being sent to Columbia, SC, a month later.

Chapter Eight

ESCAPE NO. 3

On the following day, after being thoroughly searched, I was sent to the city of Augusta and lodged in jail. Here I remained until the 7th of September when I was taken back to Macon and placed in the stockade.

Prior to our transfer to Savannah a few days later, there were about 50 officers brought in. We gave our promise not to attempt to escape if we were allowed to go outside the prison and camp in an open field. This was much pleasanter and more beneficial to our health.

On the 13th day of October, we received one day's rations and were placed aboard the cars and started for Columbia, South Carolina. We did not receive any more rations until we arrived at Columbia. We were obliged to subsist three days on six hard crackers and a small piece of bacon.

Here I found the officers I had been separated from since my first escape. We were confined in an open field guarded by about three thousand infantry and a battery of light artillery. Our treatment was very severe. A number of the prisoners were shot without any cause or provocation whatever. When I had endured the hardships of prison life in this place, I concluded to make another strike for freedom.

We made up an escape party of five and appointed Lieut. Pierson to communicate with the guard. He succeeded in bribing the guard by giving him a silver watch valued at about thirty dollars. The guard would be on duty the 19th day of November when he would be prepared to pass us through the line where he was posted. We made all necessary preparations during the day and at seven o'clock we approached the guard and succeeded in passing without creating any alarm. Our

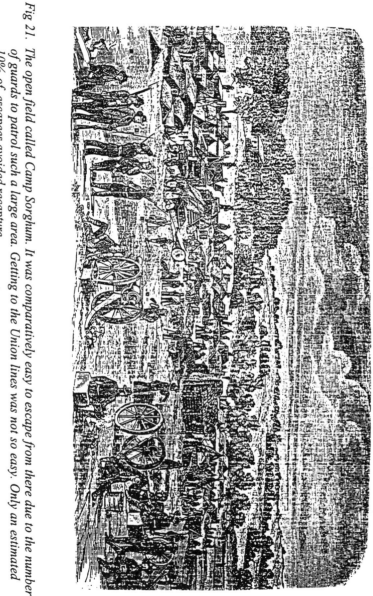

Fig 21. The open field called Camp Sorghum. It was comparatively easy to escape from there due to the number of guards to patrol such a large area. Getting to the Union lines was not so easy. Only an estimated 10% of escapees avoided recapture.

party consisted of Captain Allen, Captain Galaway, Lieutenant Stover,[12] Lieutenant Pierson, and myself.

Prior to our escape, we learned through the Rebel papers that General Sherman had vacated Atlanta and was marching in the direction of Savannah. It was generally believed among the prisoners that a portion of his army would pass through Augusta and the remainder by way of Macon. We decided to make our way to Augusta which was about 80 miles distant and secrete ourselves until the army arrived.

On the night of our escape, we walked about twelve miles and hid in the bushes about one mile west of the village of Lexington.

The next night we were overtaken by another escaped prisoner who joined our party increasing our number to six. It continued to rain all the following day. At night it grew cold. We did not dare make a fire to dry or warm ourselves for fear of being discovered. We had not gone very far when we were alarmed by the barking of dogs. While passing a house we got scattered somewhat - two of our party we lost entirely.

The next day, while sitting by our little fire, we heard somebody chopping not far distant. Supposing it to be a negro at work, Lieut. Pierson started in search of him, with a mission of procuring some rations as our supply was nearly exhausted. When he came near, he found the master there who immediately took him into his custody. He succeeded in escaping from him about 10 o'clock in the evening. He came back to the place where he had left us, but we were gone before he arrived. Now there were only three of us left.

Soon after we came onto the road in the evening, we met a Negro with a bag of corn on his back. We soon learned he was a friend to Yankees. He took us to his home and made a

---

[12] Seneca Allen, Co F; J.L.Galaway, USAAG; either J.O. Stover, 95 Ohio or M.H. Stover, 184 Pa (Both listed as POW's)

fire for us to sit by while they prepared some corn bread and sweet potatoes for us.

We got a good supply of rations and were ready to start again about two o'clock. He went with us about two miles to a secluded place where he thought we could remain in safety until the next night. We did not get much sleep as we needed to keep moving to keep warm.

After dark the Negroes came and brought us some rations. One of them went with us about two miles to assist us in finding the right road. Here we stopped at a house occupied by Negroes who were very kind to us - some of them acting as pickets while we warmed ourselves. One of the Negroes went with us into the woods about one mile where he said we would not be disturbed. He made a good fire for us and then returned to his home. We slept very well and felt much refreshed on the day following.

After dark we started on our journey again. We had not gone far when we discovered some negroes sleeping by the side of the road around a large fire. We awoke them. They informed us that they had been to Augusta with supplies for the Rebel army. They said the people were greatly alarmed, expecting the Yankee army there every day. We learned that we were only eight miles from the city. They advised us not to go too close to the city as there were pickets posted on the road.

We went about four miles farther and decided to wait until daylight and then make an effort to get across the Savannah River to the Georgia side. The river separates the states of South Carolina and Georgia. We expected that our army would approach the city on the Georgia side of the river. Our object was to cross and secrete ourselves and await the approach of the army.

We discovered some Negroes at work in a mill and, after some difficulty, we succeeded in calling the attention of one of them who came to our assistance. He informed us that his wife lived on the other side of the river and that he was allowed to go and see her occasionally. He had a canoe at the river which he used to carry himself across. He told us to come to the mill after dark. He would meet us there and convey us across the river in his canoe.

As soon as it became dark, we went to the mill according to agreement. We did not wait long before he came. After we disposed of the rations he brought us, we started for the river. We found a very difficult path. No one could have found the way if he had not been well acquainted with the country. We were obliged to cross one large stream on a fallen tree which was twelve or fifteen feet above the water. We finally arrived at the river and were soon hurried across.

He went with us until we reached the road we were to follow. He told us where to find friends to hide us and then he returned to his home.

Everything looked favorable. The Rebels were becoming much alarmed and were sending all their negroes into South Carolina to prevent their being confiscated. At this place we heard heavy cannonading which cheered us up. We hoped to be rescued very soon, but it proved to be nothing but a raiding party. They soon returned to the main army and all was quiet as ever.

When we had been there about one week, we learned that General Sherman was moving on to Savannah, leaving Augusta to his left wing. We now decided to go around to the south side of the city. We would follow the Augusta and Savannah railroad to Millen. We hoped to fall in with the army at that place. If the army had passed before we reached that point, we would follow the Central railroad to Savannah.

The second day after we left our colored friends, we secreted ourselves close by the railroad until dark. We then started in the direction of Millen which was about forty-five *miles distant. About midnight we heard some men on the road ahead of us. We immediately hid in the bushes while they passed. We concluded by their conversation that they were Negroes. Lieut. Stover followed them and hailed them, hoping to get some rations. When he came up to them, he discovered they were unarmed Rebels. They made an effort to capture him but he succeeded in extracting himself from their grasp. They followed him down the road at a double quick, but finally gave up the chase.*

Just before day we discovered a light ahead. Upon approaching it we discovered some Rebel troops encamped. We did not think it safe to follow the railroad any farther that night. We went into the woods and secreted ourselves. Just after daylight a Rebel soldier passed about one rod from us but did not discover us.

On the following morning we heard heavy firing in the direction of Waynesboro, a railroad station about four miles distant. It was an engagement between our cavalry under General Kilpatrick and Rebel cavalry under General Wheeler. After a short counsel, we decided to go around the left flank of the Rebel army and get in the rear of our army.

We had not gone very far when we discovered the Rebel troops moving about in different directions. We were obliged to secrete ourselves among the bushes to prevent being discovered by them. The engagement lasted until about noon. Our anxiety was very great. We knew we were very near our army, yet dare not make any effort to reach it.

After dark we started again. We had not gone far when we found ourselves in a dense swamp which we were unable to make our way through in the dark. We decided to wait until morning.

We started again after daylight. We found much water in the swamp, averaging from one to four feet deep. We forded in this manner until we came to a large, rapid stream called Brier

Creek. We were nearly exhausted with cold and hunger. Consequently, we did not feel able to swim the stream with our clothes on. We decided to wait until night and try to find a Negro to supply us with rations and assist us in crossing the creek.

We did not have to walk far when we came to a large plantation. While we were near the buildings watching for the Negroes, we were discovered by Rebel cavalry which we had not seen. We were obliged to surrender, as it was useless to make any resistance without arms. They were quite generous, giving us something to eat, a comfortable place to sleep, and a strong guard to watch us while we slept.

The next morning we were sent to the depot where we found a great many Rebels. They were very abusive calling us "house burners". They thought we were from General Sherman's army. We were furnished with transportation to Augusta.

On arriving at Augusta, we were immediately placed in a guardhouse which was one of the worst places I ever saw. There were nearly sixty of us forced to sleep in a room about fifteen by twenty feet. Our guards were very cruel, allowing no privileges whatever.

The following day we were placed on board the cars to Columbia where we were lodged in jail until the next morning. From there we marched into the prison from whence we had escaped three weeks previous.

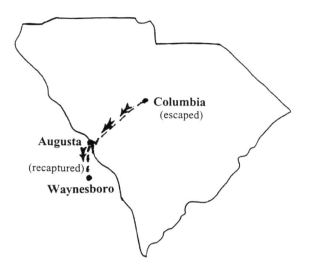

Fig 22. The route after the escape from Columbia, SC.

Lt Lafler was not alone in believing Gen Sherman's army would attempt to capture Augusta and Macon. The Confederate leaders thought so, too. They sent troops to both cities to defend them. Sherman sent cavalry units in the direction of both cities to keep the reinforcements tied up while he continued between the two cities to Savannah. It was good strategy, but bad luck for the escapees hoping to meet his forces.

The first prison in Columbia, Camp Sorghum, was essentially an open field with very little shelter. Treatment was quite severe under the command of Capt Semple, LtCol Means, and Maj Griswold.

The day after John Lafler arrived at Columbia, Oct 17, the prisoners organized a presidential election. The vote was: 1024 votes for Lincoln and 143 for McClellan. This result is interesting in that prisoners of war would so strongly back Lincoln, who proposed to fight the war to its end. They rejected McClellan, who had campaigned on the promise to compromise and end the war. The votes were mailed to Washington, but there is no verification they were received and counted.

The currency trade rate by this time had reached $20 Confederate to $1 Federal!

It was to the Confederate troops' advantage to keep the prisoners hoping to be exchanged. It was considered a "quieting powder" and reduced the desire to escape.

The morale of the guards at Camp Sorghum was very low. More prisoners, about 400, escaped from this prison than any other prison for officers in the war. Probably more would have escaped, but many had no shoes or boots. About two thirds of those escaping were recaptured. Maj Griswold, the prison commander, was formally chastised by his superiors for allowing so many escapes. His written reply complains of the lack of sufficient guards and their low morale. In one escape, three guards left with the escapees!

Capt Langworthy and Capt Aldrich from Canandaigua, NY, successfully escaped from Columbia. They headed north and met Union troops (some were from the 101st PA regiment) in Kentucky about a month later. Some escapees who had been in the 16th CT Regt at Plymouth went to the eastern shore of North Carolina where they hailed a Union blockade ship and made their escape. Reports show that all the escaping prisoners were assisted considerably by Negro slaves.

Fig 23. Five escapees from Columbia who made it back to Union lines in TN. They are, from left to right: Lt Terwilliger (Co D), Capt Aldrich (CO B), Capt Langworthy (Co E) - all from the 85th NY. The last two are: Lt Hastings (24 NY Batt) and Capt Starr (104 NY).

Chapter Nine

ESCAPE NO. 4 AND FREEDOM !!!

Our fellow prisoners joked with us about coming back so soon. We told them we only came back to get another start and that we were going through the next time.

Lieut. Pierson got back about three days sooner than we did. He was captured while attempting to cross the Savannah River near Augusta. Capt. Galaway was brought back soon after. Not one of our party succeeded in making his way out of Dixie. This was truly discouraging, but we would not give it up.

The day after our return to prison, on the ninth day of December, two hundred names were called for exchange. The men that had the most money were pretty sure to be among those to be exchanged. Those that had been in prison the longest had used most of their money, if they had had any, to buy provisions at an enormous price to keep starvation away. Therefore, they stood no chance for exchange. The only way I could get out of that horrible country was to make my escape, which I was determined to do.

On Monday, December twelfth, we received orders from the commanding officer to pack up for a move. As soon as orders came, the men set to burning their quarters. The accumulated rubbish made quite a conflagration. It was at its height as we left.

The march to the city was a perfect mob. Everybody tried to be first, hoping to get better quarters. As we passed through the city, we were paraded through the principal streets. As we passed the hotel, a Rebel was standing in front. As we came up, he opened a volley of epithets upon us. He swore he could whip the best Yankee among us. The only recognition we made of his enthusiasm were groans and a few expressions,

such as "go it old pudden head, why don't you go to the front",
etc.

When we reached the lunatic asylum, which we now
found was our destination, we were drawn up in line to listen to
a speech from Major Griswold, commander of the post. His
words were as follows: "As you enter that prison you will see a
line of barrels near the wall. That is the dead line; any man who
attempts to cross it will be shot. You will be supplied with
lumber to build barracks. The value of anything about the
grounds destroyed by you will be deducted from your money."

After the Major concluded his remarks, we were turned
into the prison. There was at once a big rush for quarters. In
less than five minutes, the only building was packed full. It could
not contain more than one hundred. Those outside were without
any shelter at all, shivering with cold and no prospect of being
better off.

On the west, in the extension of the yard, was the insane
asylum which was pretty well populated, judging from the many
doleful sounds emanating therefrom. We were separated from
the lunatics by a board fence about twelve feet high. The nights
were cold and many were obliged to run up and down the camp
to keep warm.

We were in this prison two months and, in this time,
obtained lumber enough to shelter about one fourth of our
number. That was better than we had reason to expect at their
hands.

As soon as the barracks were completed, tunneling was
commenced beneath them. We had three tunnels nearly
completed when we received orders to get ready to move again
immediately.

The next day, February 14th, we were marched to the
depot where we took transportation on the cars for Charlotte,
North Carolina arriving on the following day at about noon. We
were marched into an open field which was to be our prison.

There was no shelter of any description to protect us from the driving storms which are so frequent at that season. The recent storm had made our camp very muddy, making it rather unpleasant to sleep on the ground.

There was no water inside the lines. We were allowed to go outside the lines, in the charge of a guard, to procure water. Lieut. Pierson and I decided to take advantage of this to effect our escape. We managed to get some matches during the day and, after we received our rations, we were ready to go.

Just before dark Lieut. Pierson went out after water. He made an arrangement with a guard whereby we hoped to make our escape. After dark we were to approach the guard. Pierson was to tie a white cloth around his neck so the guard might recognize him.

He went with us to the spring. We gave him a five dollar greenback and started at a double quick. Our object was to go around the city and strike the highway east of the city. We would pursue an easterly direction until we reached the city of Newberne, situated on the Neuse River about three hundred miles distant.

We had some difficulty in finding the road as the night was very dark and cloudy and we were unable to direct our course by the stars. After we had walked a few miles we called on some Negroes who informed us that we were going too far south. They advised us to wait until the next night when they would direct us to the road. In the meantime, they would procure some rations for us.

We secreted ourselves in the woods until the following evening when we came to the house of our colored friends again. After receiving our rations, we started with one of the Negroes who acted as our guide.

The next night we made a detour to the left of the village of Monroe, the county seat, and succeeded in passing it without being discovered.

Just before day, we were challenged by some men near the road. They proved to be four prisoners who had escaped soon after we made our escape. We started with them but they were pretty noisy and we decided we would prefer trying our fortunes alone. The other party started soon after dark leaving Lieut. Pierson and myself.

While passing a house, we were attacked by three hounds. We fought them successfully with our hickory canes. After we had passed the house a little distance, the dogs retreated and we quickened our pace, fearing that we might have been discovered.

Just as daylight was making its appearance in the eastern horizon, we arrived at the shore of the big Pulec River. We were fortunate in finding a canoe chained to a tree. We confiscated it to cross the river which was about eighty rods wide at this point.

It was nearly sunrise when we reached the other side. We hastily wrapped the chain around a tree and then made our way into the woods. We were discovered in the afternoon by a black man. We learned that it was his canoe we had used. He had lent it to a man to cross the river the night before.

He informed us that we were within seven miles of the village of Rockingham, another county seat.

We were soon thirty miles from the city of Fayetteville which is located on the Cape Fear River. The country between Rockingham and Fayetteville is a barren wilderness with very few people living there. I think we passed but two or three houses in the whole distance. We got lost - otherwise we enjoyed a very quiet march.

When we arrived near a plantation, we found a number of small shanties occupied by Negroes. Lieut. Pierson went up to one of them but found that the door was locked and they would not let him in. While he was trying to tell them who we were, they threw a pan of cold water upon his head over the top of the door. We passed on to the next shanty where we found some men who let us in. They were very friendly as soon as they learned that we were Yankees. The Negroes next door thought we were deserters and so were afraid to let us in.

Lieut. Pierson's feet had become sore and we were obliged to rest a few days. Before pursuing our journey again, we slept in the house nights and secreted ourselves in the woods during the day.

Just after we went into the woods, we saw some white men approaching us. We were alarmed at first but, as they came nearer, we discovered they were escaped prisoners also. They were Capt. Cratty and Capt. Morrow of the 103rd Pa Volunteers and Capt. Cartwright and Lieut. Pitt[13] of our regiment. They had escaped soon after we had made our escape. We decided to consolidate, making a company of six.

We were engaged all night in endeavoring unsuccessfully to find some point where we might get across a stream called Rock Stream. The banks of the stream were very high and abrupt. There was no chance to get over except by a bridge, which was guarded.

On the following day we made our way back to the place we had left the previous morning. Soon after we arrived at our hiding place, one of the Negroes came to us. We told him that we wished them to assist us, if possible, in crossing the Cape Fear River. He told us to come to the house after dark and they would do the best they could for us.

When we arrived at the house, they informed us that there was a family of free negroes living about two miles away who could assist us if they would. When we arrived near that

---

[13] Alphonzo Cartwright, Co I and George Pitt, Co E

house, we stopped while Lieut. Pierson approached the house with one Negro. They came back and informed us that the man of the house was gone and nobody there except the boy and the woman. They were afraid to trust them. We went again and informed them that we were escaped prisoners. They proved to be very friendly and said they would do all they could for us. The boy said he would go with us to the river where another free man lived who would take us across the river.

We followed the boy over a very rough country but finally arrived at the house. The boy told the man what we wanted and we followed him down to the river where his canoe had been left. After we were all safely over, he went with us until we found the road and then returned home.

During the night we caught some geese. We were obliged to cook them in our cups. Consequently, we were occupied nearly all day in cooking and eating.

During the day we heard some Negroes not far from us. As soon as daylight had disappeared, Lieut. Pitt and Lieut. Pierson started in their direction to procure some rations.

We did not wait a great while before Pierson and Pitt returned with some rations. The negroes informed them that it was only twelve miles to White Hall, a small town on the Neuse River. As soon as our rations were distributed, we moved on again.

During the day we heard cannonading in the direction of the Neuse River. We supposed it to be an engagement on that road. We were acquainted with the road, having been up to White Hall about a year previous on an expedition. We were now about forty miles from Newberne.

While we were lying on the ground trying to get some sleep, a Rebel on horseback passed about five rods from us but did not discover us. We started on the following evening in the direction of Newberne, leaving Kinston to our left.

We were now obliged to be very cautious as there were likely to be scouts on the road. We decided to adopt the following plan of march so we might not all be captured if some were. Lieuts. Pitt and Pierson were to go ahead. Capt. Cartwright and myself were to follow about ten rods in the rear and Capt. Cratty and Capt. Morrow were to follow about the same distance in the rear of us.

We found that Rebels had blockaded the road at different points by felling trees across the path. We heard drums beating not more than a mile from us, but dare not approach them for fear that we might find Rebel troops instead of ours.

When we were about twenty miles from Newberne, we heard some cavalry approaching from the front. We immediately stepped off the road and hid among the trees. We were not close enough to discern their uniforms as it was pretty dark. Consequently, we were unable to make up our minds as to whether they were Yankees or Rebels. As soon as they were out of sight, we came onto the road again. By examining the tracks that the horses had made, we discovered they were shod which led us to believe they were Yankee cavalry. The Rebels seldom have their horses shod. We were determined to be very cautious and run no risk as we could not bare the thought of being captured now, after arriving so near the Union lines.

We had not gone very far when we heard more cavalry approaching. We had emerged from the woods and there was a high fence on each side of the road. Lieuts. Pitt and Pierson, who were in the advance, were discovered by the cavalry and, before they could get over the fence, they were captured.

The others of us succeeded in getting out of the road without being discovered. When we discovered ourselves safe, we listened to the conversation between those that were captured and those who had captured them. We soon learned that they had been captured by our troops. They immediately called to us. We came out and were greeted by Union soldiers again.

You cannot imagine what joy filled our bosoms as we thought of being free men once more, after suffering and enduring almost everything except death while in the hands of the Rebels.

We immediately received some rations and pursued our journey again. We reached the picket line about sunrise on the morning of the seventh day of March - three weeks after we had escaped from Charlotte, NC. We were immediately taken to the picket headquarters where we were furnished with horses to ride into the city. We reached it about noon and were greeted by many friends there.

We remained until the twelfth day of March, when we received a furlough of 30 days. We were to report to the Adjutant General immediately on arriving home. When we reached Pennsylvania, we were delayed some due to heavy rains having swollen the Susquehanna and destroying the railroad for a great distance. On the seventeenth, I was taken sick with typhoid fever.

I succeeded in reaching my home on the nineteenth day of March where I was greeted by many friends, some of whom supposed me to be numbered with the dead. They were somewhat surprised on seeing me return after an absence of three years and five months. Of that time, ten and one half months were spent in Rebel prisons.

Immediately on arriving home, I reported to the Adjutant General by letter, requesting that I be mustered out. I received my discharge dated March 21, 1865.

*I hope stern justice may overtake those **villainous traitors** who cause our prisoners to be treated in such an inhuman manner.*

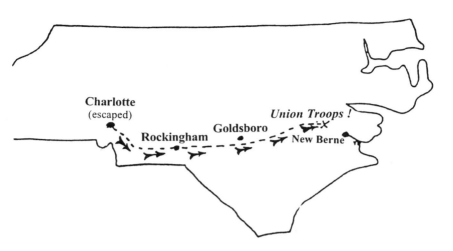

Fig 24. The route of the final, successful escape.

The men had been told they were going to Charlotte to be exchanged, but no one believed it as they had been told this so many times before. This time it was true. On February 19, four days after John Lafler escaped, the first prisoners left to be exchanged. In a twist of fate, they arrived home a week before John and his friends reached Union lines.

The Union cavalry troops to whom they surrendered were attacking from Newbern to Goldsboro.

Fig 25. This family portrait was taken in 1895 when John was 54 years old. The family members are (lt to rt): FRONT ROW - Annie, Vernon, Clay; SECOND ROW - Benjamin, John((Sr), wife Alice with Victor, Alice BACK ROW - Edwin, Floyd, Frank, John (Jr)

Chapter Ten

POST-WAR

In October, 1864, the *Albemarle* ironclad gunboat was sunk at the dock at Plymouth by a courageous night time raid. It had been damaged after the battle of Plymouth in a fight with several Union gunboats on the river. A small boat was brought within a few feet of the ironclad and a torpedo (Civil War term for an explosive mine) was exploded below the waterline and iron covering. It sank quickly and not floated again until after the war.

After the *Albemarle* was sunk, Plymouth fell to a small Union force on Oct 30, 1864. It remained in unopposed Federal control for the rest of the war.

Soon after returning home, John Lafler wrote the foregoing report of his experiences. Unfortunately, he wrote nothing of the fate of his fellow prisoners. Research has uncovered the following information about some of them.

All the 26 captured officers of the 85th NY survived the war. I have found records of escapes by 11 of them - 8 of them successfully. One group consisting of Capt Aldrich, Capt Langworthy, and 1st Lt Terwilliger escaped from Columbia and arrived home in Dec 64. 2nd Lt Welch escaped in Jan 65. John Lafler with Capt Cartwright, 2nd Lt Pierson, and 2nd Lt Pitt made their escape in Feb 65. 1st Lt Butts, the defender of Fort Williams, escaped about the same time from Charlotte, but was recaptured soon after. Capt Allen escaped with John Lafler and Lt Pierson from Columbia in Nov 64, but was recaptured with the others in Dec. He then escaped with 1st Lt Stephen Andrews but was again recaptured.

The commander, Col Fardella, was transferred with Gen Wessells from Macon to Charleston. He was paroled and sent back home in August, 1864. He returned to Sicily where he died in 1892. Capt Coats was wounded in the face at Plymouth and successfully escaped in Dec 64. Capt Raines, the first Company G commander, returned to his Geneva law practice. He was later elected to several terms to the State Assembly and Senate.

George Hainer reached the rank of sergeant before being captured and surviving the horrors of Andersonville. He was paroled on March 1, 1865. He was a neighbor and friend to John Lafler for the rest of his life.

John Lafler became a farmer after leaving the army in March, 1865. He married Alice Stern, who was nearly ten years younger, on July 3, 1866. They had eleven children: Bertie (who died at age 18), Frank, Floyd, John, Edwin, Benjamin, Clay, Vernon, Alice, Annie, and Victor. Victor was born when his father was 53 years old.

My grandfather's full name was Benjamin Gay Lafler. Among the names of men from Company G who were killed at Plymouth is the name Cpl Benjamin Gay. One wonders what circumstance led John to name a son after him. Another son, Edwin, probably was named after Lt Edwin Pierson.

Illness, probably dysentery, acquired during the Peninsula Campaign in Virginia in 1862, led to a $12 per month disability pension for John starting in 1883.

He died on November 12, 1906, at 66 years old. At the time of his death, due to "cardiac and respiratory problems", the local Penn Yan newspaper, the *Yates County Chronicle*, described him as very prosperous and said that his watchword throughout his life was "frugality". His Civil War experiences suggest "persistance" might be another one. He is buried in the Nettle Valley cemetery in the town of Potter, NY.

I think he would be pleased to know how many people, more than a century later, are interested in his wartime experiences.

APPENDIX A

BIOGRAPHICAL SKETCHES

BIOGRAPHICAL SKETCHES

Allen, Seneca (Capt)

Seneca Allen was only 21 years old when he recruited Company F of the 85th NY Regt, with the help of Stephen Andrews and Sylvenus Fay, from Black Creek, NY. He was elected Captain and commanded that company until captured at Plymouth. He organized and led several dozen civilian Negroes during the battle. He escaped with John Lafler from the prison at Columbia, but was recaptured. He and Stephen Andrews escaped later, but he was again recaptured before finally being exchanged.

Bogert, Alfred (Pvt)

Although officially reported as 18 years old when he enlisted, on roster lists his age was reported as 18(17). This implies he may have lied about his age to enlist. One of the last recruits to join prior to the regiment leaving Elmira, he died six weeks later in Washington, DC, from pneumonia. The letter from his company commander, Capt Raines to his parents notifying them of his death is in Appendix B.

Cartwright, Alphonzo (Capt)

At 22 years of age, he enrolled at Ward, NY. He was elected 1st Lt and later became a Captain and commander of Company I in November, 1863. He returned from a recruiting trip just two days before the battle of Plymouth began. One of the group of six who escaped with John Lafler, he was discharged March 22, 1865.

Fay, Sylvenus (1st Lt)

Publisher of the *Olean Times*, he and Stephen Andrews helped Seneca Allen recruit Company F. He supplied much of the financial support for which he received only partial reimbursement. He was, however, elected 1st Lt. He commanded the picket force deployed on the first day of the battle of Plymouth. He was the only "Plymouth Pilgrim" exchanged in Jan 1865, due in part to an influential friend.

Gay, Benjamin (Cpl)

Young enough to require his father's signature to enlist, Benjamin Gay was recruited for Company G during a recruiting trip in March, 1862, by George Munger. He was a Corporal when he was killed at Plymouth by a gunshot wound. John Lafler named a son after him several years later. His family received his original $100 bounty plus the $400 bounty due him for reenlisting 3 months before his death.

Hainer, George (Sgt)

Enlisting the same day and place as John Lafler, he was promoted to Corporal and then to Sergeant. He apparently upset Col Belknap as he was demoted to Private in July, 1862. He survived Andersonville, but was never healthy again. He was a friend of John Lafler before, during, and after the war.

He returned to farming after the war and died in 1900.

Munger, George (1st Lt)

He served a 3 month enlistment in a unit from Cincinnati, OH, starting in April, 1861. Returning to Penn Yan, he attempted to raise a company of volunteers, but could not attract enough recruits. He joined his with those of John Raines from Geneva and Thomas Alsop. He was wounded in the arm at Fair Oaks. Not popular with the enlisted men, he resigned in June, 1863, and became a laundry man. He died in 1919 at the age of 80 in Los Angeles, CA.

Pierson, Edwin (2nd Lt)

Mustered in on October 29, 1961, as a Corporal, he replaced John Lafler as a Sergeant, First Sergeant, and 2nd Lt. Although carried on the rolls (and paid) as a First Sergeant, he was acting 2nd Lt under John Lafler through the battle of Plymouth. He was never commissioned. He was wounded twice before surrendering at Plymouth. He spent six weeks in a hospital before going to the Macon prison. He escaped with Lt Lafler twice, including the successful one in February, 1865.

After the war he owned a nursery business in his hometown of Waterloo, NY. He died in 1914 at Santiago, Cuba, at the age of 77.

APPENDIX B

LETTERS

LETTER OF CONDOLENCE FROM CAPT RAINES TO PARENTS OF PVT BOGERT PRINTED IN THE AUG 14, 1862 EDITION OF *YATES COUNTY CHRONICLE* (Penn Yan, NY)

85th NY Vol Regt
Washington, DC
Jan 14, 1862

Mr & Mrs Bogert,
Dear Sir and Madame:

     I am called upon at this time to perform a duty the most unpleasant of any that has yet fallen to my lot as an officer, and I can only hope that the Providence which has brought this affliction upon you may comfort and sustain you in this hour of trial. It is with sorrow that I send the mournful tidings that death has invaded your family and that your son Alfred is no more. He was taken ill some two weeks since, and notwithstanding the best of care from the surgeon and his assistants, as well as his comrades who sympathise with you in this affliction, he died yesterday morning. The surgeon who had taken a great interest in Alfred will write you concerning the nature and progress of his disease.

     The funeral was attended by the Chaplain of the 77th N.Y.V. who kindly offerred to officiate, and his company followed his remains to their last resting place near the Soldier's Home, where he was buried with the honors of war. His grave is marked by a headboard on which is inscribed his name, Co, and Regt. Thus Alfred has passed away, having sacrificed his life for the honor of his country. Such is a brief history of events that has brought sorrow to your house, but let the justice of the cause which he died to sustain, and the promises of Him who doeth all things well, comfort and sustain you under this affliction.

     Your son was mustered into my Company Nov 25, and pay from that time to January 13th is due him, and $100 bounty I suppose. How this is to be obtained I will let you know as soon as I can learn. Any further information that may be desired will be gladly given.

Yours respectfully,
CAPT. J. RAINES

RESIGNATION LETTER OF 1st LT MUNGER
CO G, 85TH NY

Newberne, N.C.
Mar 30th 1863

To the Adjutant General
    Sir

    I hencewith tender my resignation as 1st Lieutenant of the 85th Reg't NYS Volunteers for the following reason viz.

    Incapacity. For a long time there has existed in the company to which I am attached a very strong dislike which has increased with, I am forced to believe, an animosity of the men of the Co., to an actual hatred toward myself. I am compelled to believe that this state of things must be caused by my incapacity, for otherwise it would not exist.

    The trials and mistipications[?] to my feelings consequent to this, with men who are far more ready and willing to disobey than to obey any commands I may give can readily be imagined and it would seem to me that I cannot be blamed for wishing to escape from them.

    I do not know that I have committed any act for which I would deserve a dismissal from the service. The want of capacity to govern and control men is something for which nature is responsible - not I. Since I have been in the service it has always been my aim and ambition to perform all of my duties to the very best of my ability. All of my efforts however to be of use seem to have been abortive, and since I have neither authority or influence, it is best that I be discharged. I therefore request an immediate and honorable discharge from the military service of the United States.

I am, Sir, Very Respectfully,
    Your most obedient servant,
        Geo. M. Munger
        1st Lieut., Co. G, 85th Regent, NYS Vols

EXCERPTS FROM LETTERS FROM
CAPTAIN NELSON CHAPIN, COMPANY K
85th REGIMENT AT 85th REDOUBT, PLYMOUTH

Oct. 4th, 1863

My Dear Wife:

Our camp is still in the same place as when I last wrote you. I have two guns mounted on our fort, though the fort is not yet completed. We work on it all we are able to for Co. K and Co. E united have no day 10 men (Privates) that are not excused from duty and as our detail for guard should be six each day you see it brings the men on just about every day and not enough to fill our details at that: there is no man that I know of dangerously sick. Ague and fevers are the order of the day. Every precaution is used by officers to care for their men that can possibly be used: yet duty is duty and nothing but the decision of the surgeons can exempt a man from it. My own health is pretty good and as every man of our officers are unfit for duty, my labors for some time have asked me to the uttermost but I am very thankful I am able to do it. One day Gen. Officer of the Day and ride to the picket lines and along the whole length of them (ten to twelve miles) on the gallop stopping a moment to give orders at each post. This in the morning and again a little before night to give out the countersign and then after midnight the grand rounds. The Gen. Officer of the Day has a cavalry man with him for orderly. Next day Regt. Officer of the Day: next day Post Officer of the Day and so we go.

The Rebels launched their iron clad ram up the Roanoke one week ago last Friday and I think will be down here by and by with that and a land force and make a combined attack on us by sea and land and if no iron clad is sent us, there is a good chance we have all we can attend to.

Good night. "Capt. Chapin is Officer of the Day" tomorrow, was yesterday and came off at 10 A.M. today.

N. CHAPIN

NELSON CHAPIN LETTERS (cont'd)

Nov. 5, 1863

My Dear Son,

  We are still in the same camp as when I last wrote you. I lead my company and one more, the rest of our Regiment is back one mile and in town. We have a little fort here of which I am in command. We have but two guns mounted but Maj. Gen. Peck told me he would send me a rifled gun, 32 pounder. I shall mount it as to sweep all points of the compass. I have been building a magazine and deepening the ditch around the fort and other things which have kept me very busily employed for the last two months and I am still at work and have come to the conclusion that a fort is like farm work, never completed. Our post is about a half mile from and overlooking the Roanoke River and is on the extreme right flank and about one mile from any other work or fortification except that there is a breast work for riflemen 3/4 mile in our rear so you can see that in case of an attack on our post, our fort will be the first to be struck at as ours flanks the front of Fort Williams and that at one mile and commands the front of one half mile more. Gen. Peck told me I had the Post of Danger. I told him it is the Post of Honor and I wished to hold it. We have an Italian, a Sardinian, Col. for our Col. He is very friendly to me, uses me with marked consideration, is very kind to me all which I value more for the influence it may and will give me to serve you and he has promised me that he will nominate you to Gov. Seymour for a commission in our Regt. It is now sixteen months since I have seen any of my family, have been in three battles and under fire three times more in that time and have not received a single scratch and not a scar. My health remains excellent as a general thing.

       Your Father,
       NELSON CHAPIN

2nd MASS HEAVY ARTILLERY AT FORT GRAY, PLYMOUTH, NC

March 25, 1864

My Dear Parents:

I have a little time to write to you tonight. Your letters are very welcome. I believe the last time I wrote I told you there was no chance for a fight. I am now almost convinced that we shall have a muss before long. The ram is on the river and my fort will be the first object of attack if she comes. God grant that she don't get any farther, and that I be able to do my full duty. I hope that she will come if they will only let me fight her alone but if they insist on bringing in a land force of artillerists and sharp-shooters with them to keep us away from our guns, it will be very unpleasant. I shall have some of the "Secret Service" business so much thought of to tell about when the war is over. I wish you could be here when some of the refugees and escaped prisoners come in. Four came in a few days since who had escaped from the cars while on the way to Georgia from Richmond. They were a whole fortnight in the woods and, what is now agreed upon by all, they testified that every negro they saw was faithful to them, that when they found they were Union soldiers they would feed them and conceal them, act as their guides and risk their lives for them. You should have seen those men, their voices so full of happiness and their eyes full of tears as they looked at the old flag. They had queer stories of their adventures to tell. One of them concealed a $50 bill in a button, another a gold watch in his shirt-tail and they told these things in their rich Irish way that was perfectly irresistible.

I have had a good deal of company today and feel quite jovial.

I have been listening to a negro preacher tonight who thinks he is "gifted" and will give a full account of him in some future letter.

For the present, in the best of health and gayest of spirits, I am, I hope,

Your dutiful and loving son,
JOSEPH E. FISKE

OFFICIAL REPORT OF 1 LT LUCIEN BUTTS CONCERNING SURRENDER OF FT WESSELLS (85th REDOUBT)

April 1, 1865

GENERAL:

I have the honor, at this earliest practicable time after my release from prison, to report the operation at the 85th Redoubt, Plymouth, NC, preceding the surrender of that work, April 18, 1864, the command, by the mortally wounding of Capt Chapin, having fallen upon me as senior officer present.

The garrison of the redoubt consisted of 42 enlisted men of Company K, 85th NY Volunteers, with its officers, Capt N Chapin, Lt LA Butts, and 2nd Lt SS Peake, and 23 enlisted men of Company H, 2nd Mass Heavy Artillery, commanded by 2nd Lt HL Clark. Its armament was a light 32 pounder on a ship carriage, and an old pattern iron 6 pounder field piece. Occasional shots were made from our guns as parties of the enemy made their appearance in the vicinity of Washington road after our pickets were driven in on the evening of the 17th and the morning of the 18th. About 10 am of the 18th three rifled guns opened fire from near the Fagan house upon our pickets near the redoubt, replying also to our guns. During two hours or more good practice was apparently made by our 32 pounder against these guns. Nod damage was done to the redoubt, though several shells struck it. Firing was discontinued during the greater part of the afternoon until near night, when a few shells were thrown upon the line of battle advancing upon our skirmishers between the Washington and Long Acre roads. While our attention was drawn in this direction, a battery was brought into position in the field on the southern front of the redoubt, which opened a rapid fire before our large gun could be shifted to bear upon it. The 6 pounder only could be used but was well served under a close fire, two of the infantry helping to man it at the last in place of the artillery who failed to come to the work. One of its earliest discharges exploded a caisson. Under cover of the fire of this battery, and nearly hidden in the obscurity of the night by the ground descending toward the swamp and by the proximity of the woods, a heavy column of infantry was advanced to assault the redoubt. This column was

opened upon by our musketry when about 160 yards distant, but
it advanced steadily and soon enveloped the redoubt on every
side, pouring in a heavy fire. The abatis was soon penetrated,
when hand grenades were used by us, apparently with good
effect, as the attacking force soon retired, to rally again,
however, in a short time. This was three or four times repeated,
but with little order or success in getting through the abatis. The
enemy finally passed in line toward the town, leaving some
stragglers in our vicinity. 26 of these, some of them wounded,
but mostly unhurt, surrendered in small squads, and were
assisted to scale the walls into the redoubt. Our loss in repelling
this assault was 1 killed and 3 wounded (3 mortally). The
wounded included the only competent gunners fit for duty.

After an interval of about half an hour, several guns
opened upon the redoubt from a knoll about 250 yards from the
south wall, and two or three guns at a distance of 100 yards,
opposite the southwest corner, the fire from the two positions
crossing at a right angle. The last named guns were placed under
the bank of the swamp, so that neither of ours could bear upon
them. The darkness prevented the enemy from being seen while
placing his guns, and an attempt to use our field piece where a
movement could be heard was abandoned after one or two
discharges as useless. The enemy's sharpshooters were active
while their batteries played upon the redoubt. The small building
in the corner of the work, upon which the fire was concentrated,
proved a source of great danger. The percussion shells from the
enemy's guns struck its roof and chimney, exploding and
sending deadly missiles to nearly every part of the redoubt. Capt
Chapin was struck by a fragment of one of these shells during
the second cannonade, about 9:30 o'clock. The fire was also
very effective upon the walls of the redoubt, penetrating deep
and throwing off much earth by the explosions. The sandbags
were broken and thrown off the parapet, so as to destroy the
loophole on the sides of attack. After the second cannonade had
been some time continued, fire was opened in that direction by
our gun boats, but their shells passed over and exploded far
beyond the enemy's batteries. Some shells from the town
seemed to be better elevated and better timed, but were without
apparent effect. The last two shells from the gunboats struck and
exploded, one on the parapet, the other upon the traverse
covering the door of the magazine, both in perfect range for the
magazine. Shortly after, the firing ceased and demand was made

for a surrender. The officers present, including Capt Chapin, were consulted before replying. A large force was known to be between the redoubt and the town, cutting off communication. The cartridges were nearly expended, only half a dozen grenades were left, our gunners were disabled, the prisoners were a great embarrassment; there were no means of spiking the guns or of making signals. There appeared in the darkness no hope of efficient help from the gunboats or from the town batteries, and the fire received from the gunboats, if repeated, left no safe place in the work. It was unanimously decided to be a useless waste of life to continue the contest longer, and that it was best to surrender. Possession of the work was given about 11 PM.

The total casualties of Co K, 85th NY Volunteers, were Capt N. Chapin mortally wounded, 1 sergeant killed, and 3 other enlisted men wounded (1 mortally); and of Co H, 2nd Mass Heavy Artillery, 6 wounded (2 supposed mortally).

I cannot speak too highly of the spirit and conduct of the men of my own company, to whom, in the subordinate position I held during the greater part of the engagement, my attention was principally confined. No fear of their readiness to fight as long as required was among the considerations leading to the surrender. Wagoner Dana Allen and Private Nason Chase were especially worthy of praise for their bravery in helping to man the guns when partially deserted, the first, after he was himself wounded.

For the details of the operations of the artillery of the redoubt, and a report of the conduct of the men of that service, I refer you to the report of Lt Clark.

I am able to learn no more of Capt Chapin after he was left in care of the enemy than that he died at some temporary hospital, or on his way to one, before morning.

The force making the assault was Kemper's brigade and the 21st GA Regiment, all led by Col Mercer, of the 21st GA, who was killed before the redoubt. We were told that the enemy lost before the redoubt 60 in killed alone, and a large number wounded. Appearances in the vicinity, so well as we could judge in the darkness, indicated that they had lost severely.

Very respectfully, your obedient servant,

L.A. BUTTS
1st Lieutenant 85th NY Volunteers

LETTER BY CAPT. M. LYNCH, 21st GEORGIA REGIMENT IN FRONT OF PLYMOUTH, NC

April 19, 1864

Dear Sir:

A few days back we left our camp at Kinston, and marched to attack the enemy at Plymouth, NC. On reaching there we found him strongly fortified, but the attack was ordered and made on yesterday the 18th. It was a brilliant charge, but sad to tell many brave and noble youths lost their lives. And foremost among the brave and gallant band who gave their lives for their country, I am pained to say, was your son Sidney. He fell in the chase about dark yesterday evening, shot through - the ball taking effect in the left breast. Next day his remains were taken charge of by James B. May and buried. He marked a head board with his name, all that by sympathy and affection could do him was done. I deeply regret the necessity which called forth these lines notifying you of the death of your son but it is not for us to repine. We must submit to the will of Him who gives and can take away.

I must say that a truer, nobler, or more generous youth has not fallen in this cruel and unnatural war, would to God, he had been spared to his country and to you.

Very respectfully,
M. LYNCH

LETTER BY BENJAMIN G. JONES, 21st GEORGIA REGT AT FORT WILLIAMS

April 21, 1864

My Dear Brother:

After eating a hearty supper such as sugared coffee, bacon and chicken and pushing back my plate and taking a light, I will tell you of our late battle at this place. On the 13th of this month we took the cars at Kinston. On the morning of the 14th we arrived at Tarboro and took up march for this place and on the 17th we reached their picket lines and took them on surprise we captured some of them though the reserve made their escape and gave the alarm.

When we reached the town we formed a line of battle within one mile and a half of the town and lay quiet until the morning of the 18th when a severe artillery fight took place. The enemy were well fortified and had three forts built and three gunboats to support them and on the morning of the 19th our regiment and the 21st North Carolina was drawn up in line to charge one of the forts which had three seige pieces in it and a good many infantry. Our Colonel was acting Brigidier General - the charge was ordered and the men went like a thunder storm and yelling like so many wild beasts they soon reached the fort through a storm of grape shots and cannister - the fort had brush around it and every limb sharpened and next to the fort a ditch was near ten feet deep which made the fort near twenty five feet high - the most of the boys made their way through the brush and got to the fort, but the ditch being so deep and the fort so steep not many men could reach the top. The enemy stopped firing of their guns but threw hand grenades over the fort which exploded very rapidly amongst the men - our flag reached the fort and was planted on it and they struck at it with their guns and tore it nearly in two. They finally surrendered. Our Colonel was killed, Colonel Mercer, and Wiley W. Carter of our company was mortally wounded who has died since, Milford Wiley very badly wounded in the shoulder and one or two slightly wounded.

Our gun boat ran down the river of the enemy and sunk one gun boat and one transport and came vey near sinking two more. They went off in a sinking condition. We then had the enemy surrounded and commenced seige on the other two forts which they soon ceased to fire and surrendered. We took twenty five hundred prisoners and I think thirty pieces of artillery and enough commissaries to do us four or five months. All of their tents fell into our hands though they are badly torn up. The tent that I am in has more than a hundred holes in it. Our Brigidier General commanded the fight. - we had only three Brigadiers. This place had been a beautiful town though badly torn up now. The river is called Roanoke and ia a very long river. Our Regiment is staying in the town and a portion of them in the fort. My quarters is within ten steps of Fort Williams. We are living fit now have most anything to eat that we want. I know not how long we will remain here but I suppose until we rest. Think as soon as we get well rested we will try a place near this called Washington and if we succeed we will have a fine time. I think we will soon have North Carolina cleaned of all Yankees.

I would be happy to receive a letter. Write as soon as you receive this and let me know the news. Tell Elizabeth to write.

I forgot to tell you the name of the place that is taken. It is Plymouth.

Your brother,

BENJAMIN G. JONES

P.S. I am writing by candle light and all the boys is snoring fast asleep.

APPENDIX C

BIBLIOGRAPHY

Books

Barrett, J   *Civil War In North Carolina* (Chapel Hill: Univ
        of NC Press, 1990)
Cooper, A   *In and Out of Rebel Prisons* (Oswego, NY: RJ
        Oliphant, 1884)
Davis, G   *The Official Military Atlas of the Civil War* (NY:
        Gramercy, 1983)
Davis, W   *Fighting Men of the Civil War* (New York:
        Smithmark Publishers, 1993)
Denney, R   *Civil War Prisons and Escapes* (New York:
        Sterling Publishing Co, 1993)
Elliott, R   *Ironclad of the Roanoke* (Shippensburg, PA:
        White Mane Publishing Co, 1994)
Geer, J   *Behind the Lines* (Philadelphia, PA: JW
        Daughaday, 1864)
Iobst, R   *The Bloody Sixth* (Gaithersburg, MD: Olde
        Soldiers Books, 1965)
Jordan, W   "Massacre at Plymouth" - *North Carolina Review*
        (April 1995) pg 125 - 197
Kellogg, R   *Life and Death in Rebel Prisons* (Hartford CT:
        L Stebbins, 1867)
Lamont, D   *War of the Rebellion: Official Records* Series II
        (Washington, DC: GPO, 1894)
Langworthy, G *Reminiscences of a Prisoner of War and His
        Escape* (Minneapolis, MN: Byron Printing, 1915)
Mahood, W   *Charlie Mosher's Civil War* (Hightstown, NJ:
        Longstreet House, 1994)
Mahood, W   *The Plymouth Pilgrims* (Hightstown, NJ:
        Longstreet House, 1991)
Reed, J   *History of the 101st PA Regt 1861 - 1865*
        (Chicago, IL: LS Dickey, 1910)
Urban, J   *Battle Field and Prison Pen* (Washington, DC:
        Hubbard Bros, 1887)
White, H   *Prison Life Among the Rebels* (Kent, OH: Kent
        State University Press, 1990)
Wiley, B   *The Life of Billy Yank* (Baton Rouge, LA:
        Louisiana State University Press, 1978)
----------   *Revised Regulations for the Army of US 1861*
        (Philadelphia, PA: JGL Brown, 1861)

Letters, Articles, Unpublished Documents

History of the Black Creek Co, !st Lt Fay, Co F, 85th NY Regt

The Fall of Plymouth, Comm Sgt N. Lanpheur, 85th NY Regt

My Life in Dixie, 1st Lt J Lafler, Co G, 85th NY Regt

Yates County Chronicle, 1862, Letters: Capt J Raines
                                        1st Lt G Munger

Letters: 1st Lt S Andrews
         Capt N Chapin
         Pvt B Jones
         Capt M Lynch
         Pvt G Rogers

Report by Wm Smith, Surgeon, 85th NY Regt